Cotton and Wool
Miss Jump's Farewell

By Linda Brannock

Cotton and Wool
Miss Jump's Farewell
By Linda Brannock

Editor: Deb Rowden
Designer: Kelly Ludwig
Photography: Aaron T. Leimkuehler
Illustration: Lon Eric Craven
Technical Editor: Barbara Nesemeyer
Production assistance: Jo Ann Groves

Published by:
Kansas City Star Books
1729 Grand Blvd.
Kansas City, Missouri, USA 64108

First edition, first printing
ISBN: 978-1-933466-39-2

Library of Congress Control Number: 2007930958

Printed in the United States of America by Walsworth Publishing Co., Marceline, MO

To order copies, call StarInfo at (816) 234-4636 and say "Books."

 KANSAS CITY STAR BOOKS

The Quilter's Home Page

www.PickleDish.com

KANSAS CITY STAR QUILTS
Continuing the Tradition

Contents

All designs by Linda Brannock. Photos on the preceding pages were shot on location at Linda's home. Linda is pictured with Rita Briner, an old friend and one of her first students.

Dedication

To my husband of 50 years, Robert H. Brannock, Sr. Thanks for building me a great studio and doing all the cooking since you retired (we are really not this old!).

Acknowledgements

Rita Briner, for motivation, friendship and quilting.
Debbie Lillich, for hooking the rug.
Tami Watson, for great quilting.
Janice Johnson, Rita Briner and Debbie Lillich: for making memory boxes.
Becky Dye, for piecing Easy Stars.

Introduction

Primitive and Perfection

To me, primitive is not a lack of knowledge or craftsmanship. It is a more relaxed style. Not rigid, not sloppy. Primitive is mixing plaids, prints stripes and checks in a relaxed way. Your mother would never have let you leave the house if your clothes were mixed in this way. The craftsmanship can be just as good as any museum quilt, the corners just as square, the borders just as straight and the stitches just as precise.

It is like the difference between folk art and fine art - country music and opera.

—Linda Brannock

About the Author

This all started when I wanted a quilt. In 1974, there were not many for sale and not any that I could afford. So I knew I would have to make one. Finally, I found a class and began this great journey.

I started teaching in 1980, to a group of friends in my basement. After practicing on friends, I taught at eight different places and traveled 200 miles a week.

I created patterns for local businesses: Quilt Country, then Evening Star Farm, Red Wagon and now for Quilter's Station. I have loved the last 27 years - many joys and stresses. I've enjoyed traveling, teaching, attending quilt markets all over the U.S., and designing fabric for Moda.

I started my own pattern business, the Star Quilt Company, in 1993 and loved it for 10 years.

I've decided it's time to retire—to bid farewell to Miss Jump and the quilt business. What am I going to do now? PLAY…….. with Sugar; in my very overgrown garden… I'm sure I will play with fabric, as I have since I was about 8 years old. But now it will be with no deadlines—and no writing instructions.

Linda, 9, swings sister Katie in the garden in their backyard.

About Miss Jump

I grew up in a most wonderful neighborhood in Independence, Missouri. All the houses were very different, as were the occupants. I was very intrigued by Miss Jump. She built her own house like in Hansel and Gretel, far back from the street with many flowers and shrubs. You could barely see her small house. She was always working in her garden and Miss Jump was interested in all the children in the neighborhood. She was an "old maid" and had taught school. I loved to be invited in for tea. Her house was like a doll house inside - so small and with such lovely things - china cups and saucers with tiny flowers on them, a canary in a white cage, flowered wallpaper and crochet pieces on the arms and backs of chairs (I know this crochet piece has another name - it is antimacassar). Much time was spent making them and washing and starching them.

I always thought her grounds were full of weeds because you could barely see the small cottage. Now I know them as perennials. I never saw Miss Jump in her garden without her sunbonnet and a starched and ironed house dress on. What else would a lady wear – always a dress. My grandmother told me Miss Jump hated to start building her house because the bluebirds were nesting there. She always hoped they would return.

Gossip

When I was teaching my friends, there was one who needed me to thread a bunch of needles each week at class. When she ran out of those, she quit until the next week.

One time a bunch of friends were quilting at my home. We were having a great time. When they left, we noticed the sun was rising.

I took painting classes for about 24 years. You would think I am a great painter - you would be wrong. But we had much fun. One of the ladies in class brought a quilt of pieced ladies heads and arms that she had bought at a garage sale. She let me borrow it to show at guild and I returned it. Barbara Brackman borrowed it for an article and called it "Linda Brannock's Baldheaded Lady". I probably borrowed it from my friend at least seven times. She said when she has the quilt it goes on a closet shelf, but when I have it lots of people get to see it and she gave it to me. I treasure it. Thank you again, Edna.

I have a very good friend of a great many years. I will call her A. She and I were invited to a very special home by a lady and her daughter for lunch and to see their great old home. At lunch, we were served tuna sandwiches and ice tea. It was really a dark tuna but it had pickles, mayo and onions. I figured it was not albacore which is what I always get. So I drank a lot of tea to wash down each bite. So did A. The daughter says "Mom, I think you mixed up the tuna with the cat food tuna." Well, she said no way, but I was sure that was true. We weren't there much longer and I haven't eaten tuna since and that was 18 years ago.

A was also with me when I went to pick up an antique cupboard I had purchased out in the country. We really thought we could get it in the car/wagon. Did I say it was raining? Did I say they had a bunch of baby kittens about six weeks old and they wanted in the car out of the rain? What a picture we must have made - three middle-aged women, a cupboard in our hands and kittens jumping in and out of the car. Of course, the cupboard did not fit. The antique lady felt so bad. They delivered the cupboard that evening and I still have it.

A (my friend) went to an auction early one morning with her hubby and it was squishy/muddy. He was going to wipe off her shoes when they got back to the car and she sat on the seat. He started laughing. The shoes didn't match and not only that, they had different size heels.

General Instructions

All pattern pieces and measurements need to have 1/4" seam allowance added unless otherwise stated. Pattern lines are the sewing line, not the cutting line.

Fabric

Use 100% cotton fabric whenever possible. If you must purchase a blend because it is the perfect print, make sure it is a least 60% cotton. Wash the fabric before using it. When washing darks or reds, add a cheap white terry washcloth to the load. If the cloth is not white after the washing, find out which piece 'bled' and rewash it, then add a cup of vinegar to the rinse water. Dry in the dryer, press if necessary.

Thread

Use 100% cotton or cotton covered polyester thread for piecing and appliqué. Quilting thread should be 100% cotton when possible (white or off white).

Batting

I prefer a fairly thin batt with a high percentage of cotton.

Scissors

Use one pair for template material and another sharp pair for fabric only.

Templates

Use clear or frosted plastic sheets sold for this purpose or poster board.

Marking Surface

Glue #180 sandpaper to the back of a desk mat or compressed board. This will keep your fabric secure when marking. Mark on the right side of fabric for appliqué and the wrong side of fabric for piecing. A small r after the letter or number of a template means to reverse the piece by turning the template over.

Seam Allowance

All seam allowances are 1/4".

Single Binding

★ Seam allowance is included in these measurements. Cut on the straight of the fabric. Cut 2 strips 1" by the width of quilt plus 5".

★ Cut 2 strips 1" by the length of quilt plus 5".

★ Pin the right side of the binding to the right side of the quilt, leaving 2 1/2" extra binding at each end. Stitch the binding in place through the front of quilt, batting and backing. Sew all 4 borders, making sure the stitches meet at the corners. If stitches do not meet, correct with hand stitches. Miter the corners, hand sew the miter, trim and turn. Turn back 1/4" seam allowance on the raw edge and stitch. Sign and date your work.

Double Binding

This is a double binding used mainly for quilt size projects that might get more wear. Seam allowances are included in these measurements.

★ Cut on the straight of fabric.

★ Cut 2 strips 2 1/8" by the width of the quilt.

★ Cut 2 strips 2 1/8" by the length of the quilt.

★ Press binding in half, wrong sides together so it is 1 1/16" wide.

★ Pin the raw edges of binding to the right side of the quilt, leaving 2 1/2" extra binding at each end. Stitch through:

1) both layers of binding
2) front of quilt
3) batting, and
4) backing.

★ Sew binding to all 4 sides, making sure the stitches touch at the corners. If stitches do not meet, hand sew the corners so they do. Miter the corner, hand sew the miter, trim and hem. Stitch the folded edge of the binding to the back of the quilt.

★ Sign and date your work.

Pineapple
Size: 52" x 52"

Requirements

- ★ 2 yards fabric light background
- ★ 3/4 yard black fabric for sawtooth and inner borders
- ★ 1/2 yard red dot fabric for hearts
- ★ Fat quarters – gold plaid, green dot and gold check for pineapples, stars, moon, star tops
- ★ 1 1/2 yards black for outside border and binding

Instructions

- ★ Use the same pineapple and star templates in the Pineapple tablerunner.
- ★ The 4 block backgrounds are cut 21" square.
- ★ Mark from center corner (pick one) 7 3/4" and that is the placement for the center sawtooth.
- ★ Cut 4 pineapples, 4 star tops and 4 sawtooth corners. The pineapple tucks under the sawtooth.
- ★ Cut 7 hearts and 1 moon (refer to photo).

Borders

- ★ The inner border is 2" wide. Cut 4 – 2" x 2" cornerstones of red to add to this border.
- ★ The outside border is 4" wide.

About Pineapples

I just finished my seventh pineapple quilt. I love the graphics of repeat pineapple blocks and this will probably not be my final one. This addiction could be cured if I could live in Hawaii on a permanent basis. We were there one January and to wake up in the morning with the windows open and the beautiful birds singing was quite a thrill. We saw doves that are completely different than the ones in our backyard.

Our son took us to all the tourist places in and around Honolulu, including Dole pineapple farms. I don't know how I imagined pineapples grew, but these sure looked fake. They looked like cheap plastic fruit poked up on a very straight stem. I checked it out and they were real. This past summer our son brought us two cases of sugar loaf pineapples and of course he fed them to everyone who visited us, including the Liberty Gathering tour.

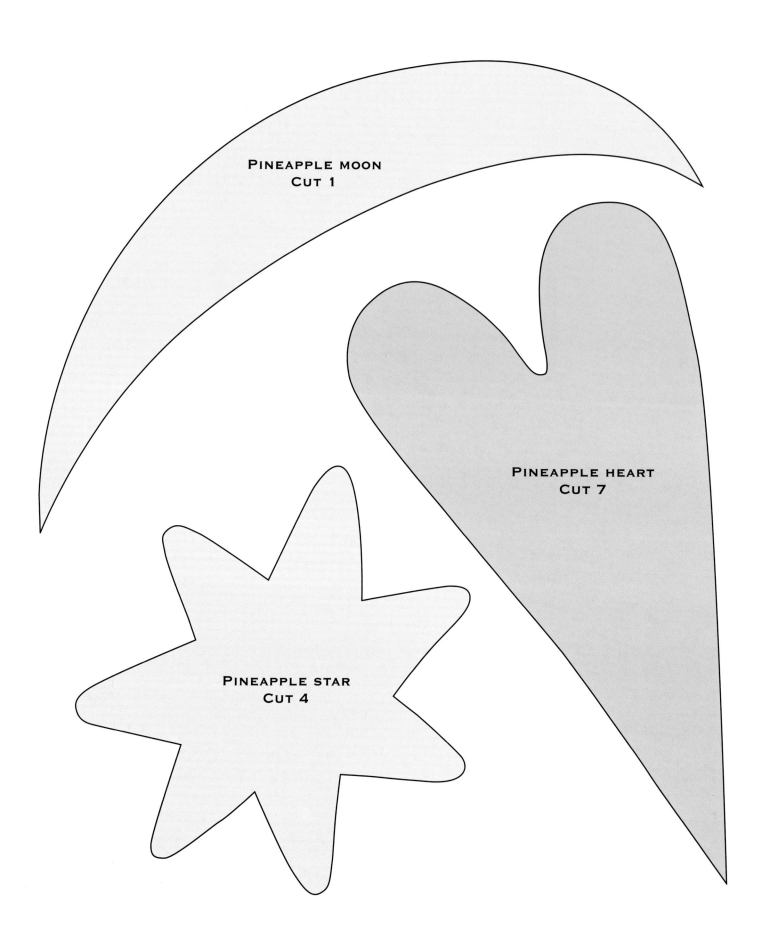

PINEAPPLE MOON
CUT 1

PINEAPPLE HEART
CUT 7

PINEAPPLE STAR
CUT 4

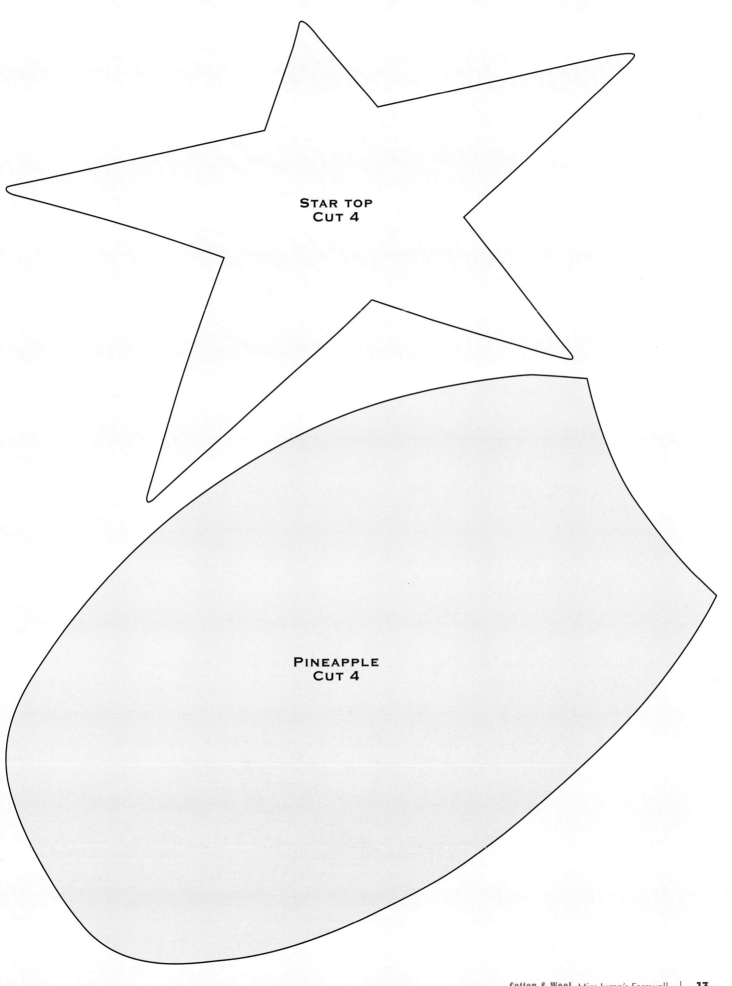

STAR TOP
CUT 4

PINEAPPLE
CUT 4

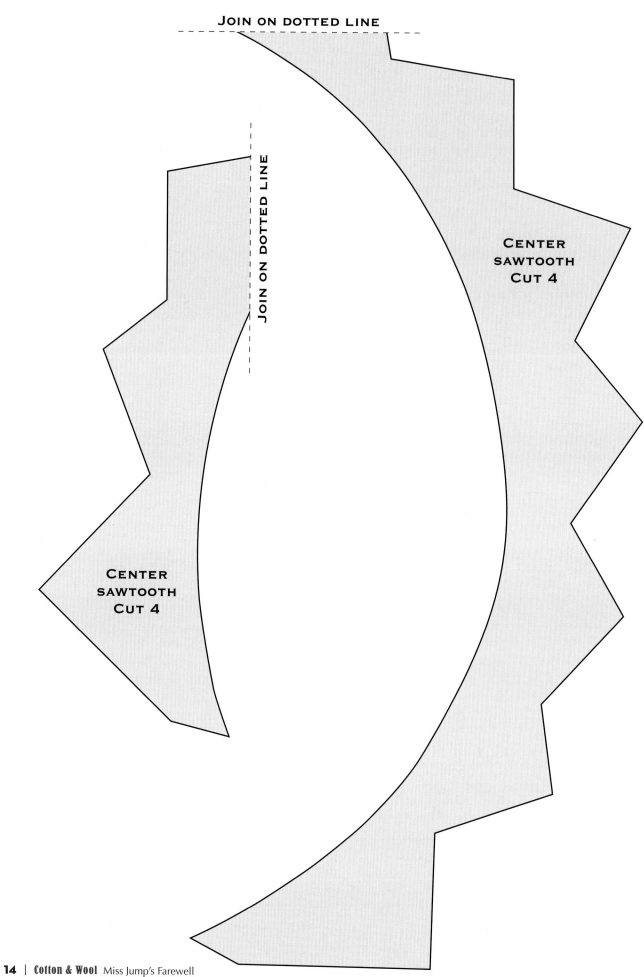

JOIN ON DOTTED LINE

JOIN ON DOTTED LINE

CENTER SAWTOOTH CUT 4

CENTER SAWTOOTH CUT 4

JOIN ON DOTTED LINE

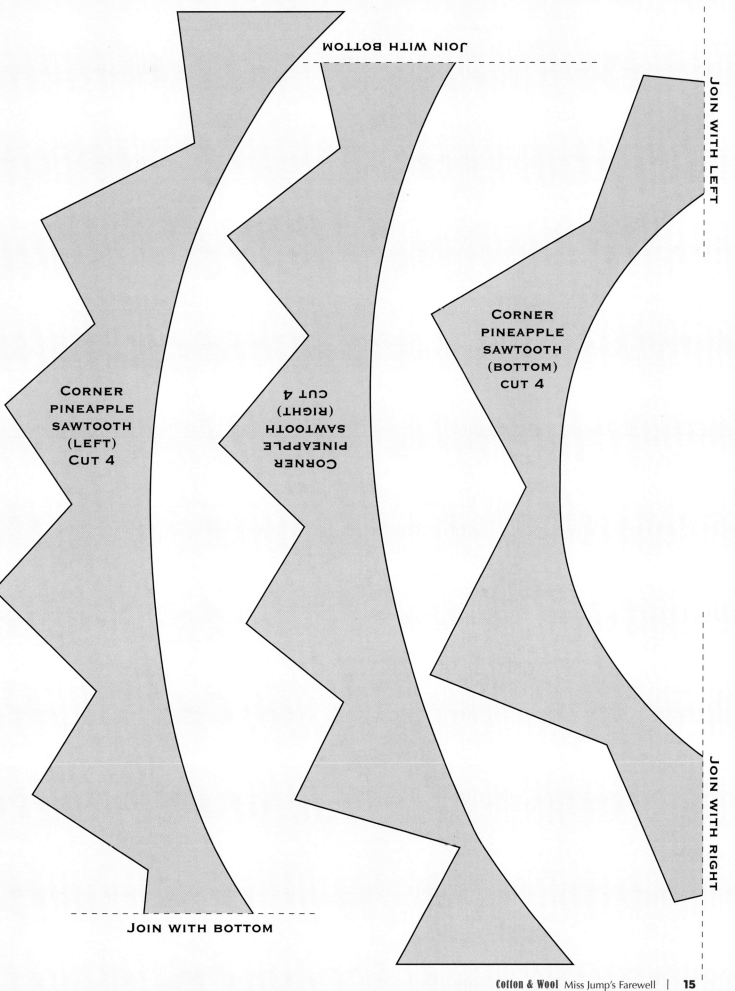

CORNER PINEAPPLE SAWTOOTH (LEFT) CUT 4

CORNER PINEAPPLE SAWTOOTH (RIGHT) CUT 4

CORNER PINEAPPLE SAWTOOTH (BOTTOM) CUT 4

JOIN WITH BOTTOM

JOIN WITH LEFT

JOIN WITH RIGHT

JOIN WITH BOTTOM

American Beauty
Size: 56" x 68"

Requirements

★ 18 fat quarters for light backgrounds

★ 1 3/4 yard star fabric for border and binding

★ 1/2 yard total of reds for small and large buds

★ 1/2 yard red with green dots for center flower circle and hearts

★ 1 yard green dot for stems

★ 1/2 yard solid green for double leaves and center flower petals

My Garden

I started my garden seven years ago so I could have "vases full" of flowers in my home. That was my goal. So far, I have had two. When something looks great in the garden, I hate to cut it down and put it inside where it will last only a few days. In the garden, it has a chance of lasting two weeks or more—so I guess I need to plant by the masses. Then maybe I could cut 10 stalks of flowers and they wouldn't be missed. I thought this was going to be SO simple.

Instructions

Piecing the background

- ★ Cut a 4″ strip x width of fabric from each light background. (A)

- ★ Piece these together on the long side in rows of 3 and then cut again into 4″ strips. (B)

- ★ Sew together enough to make 8 nine–patch blocks.

- ★ See diagram of other blocks to make. (C)

- ★ Sew these blocks together: 4 across and 5 down.

Appliqué

- ★ Flowers: Appliqué the 4 circles with the sawtooth circle (see pattern on page 20) on top. Trim out excess fabric behind the circles.

- ★ Add the small circle to the center and trim out behind. Position the 4 flowers.

- ★ Stems: The stems are cut approximately 1 1/2″ wide. Some of the smaller stems going to the red buds (see pattern on page 19) are cut 1″ wide. *I do not like my stems to be cut perfect. I cut them freehand.*

- ★ Cut 4 stems 25″ long and position under flower and to the corner of the quilt. Don't appliqué until everything is in place.

- ★ Cut 4 outside V stems 44″ x 1 1/2″. The center of this stem covers the stem from the flower head. They end 1″ from center seam and 2 1/4″ from the edge of the quilt.

- ★ Appliqué the double leaves and hearts next.

- ★ Position stems and buds along the main stem, referring to the photo for placement.

- ★ The outside border is 4″ wide.

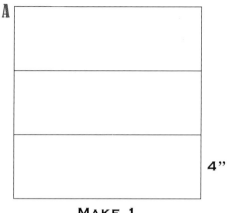

A

4″

MAKE 1

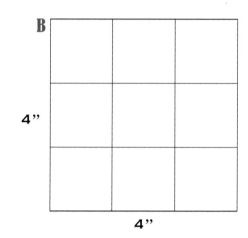

B

4″

4″

MAKE 7

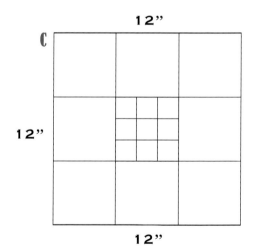

C

12″

12″

12″

MAKE 1

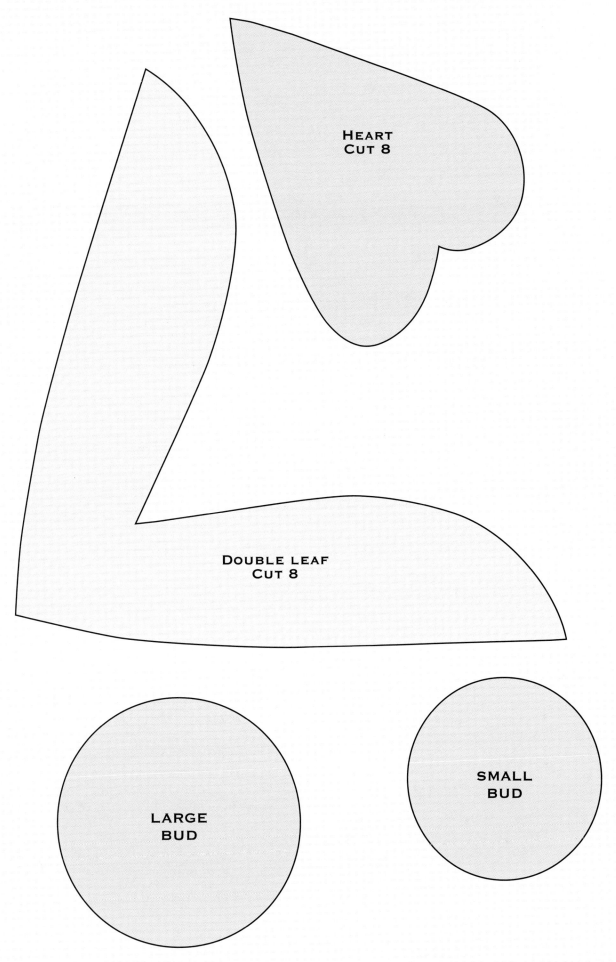

HEART
CUT 8

DOUBLE LEAF
CUT 8

LARGE
BUD

SMALL
BUD

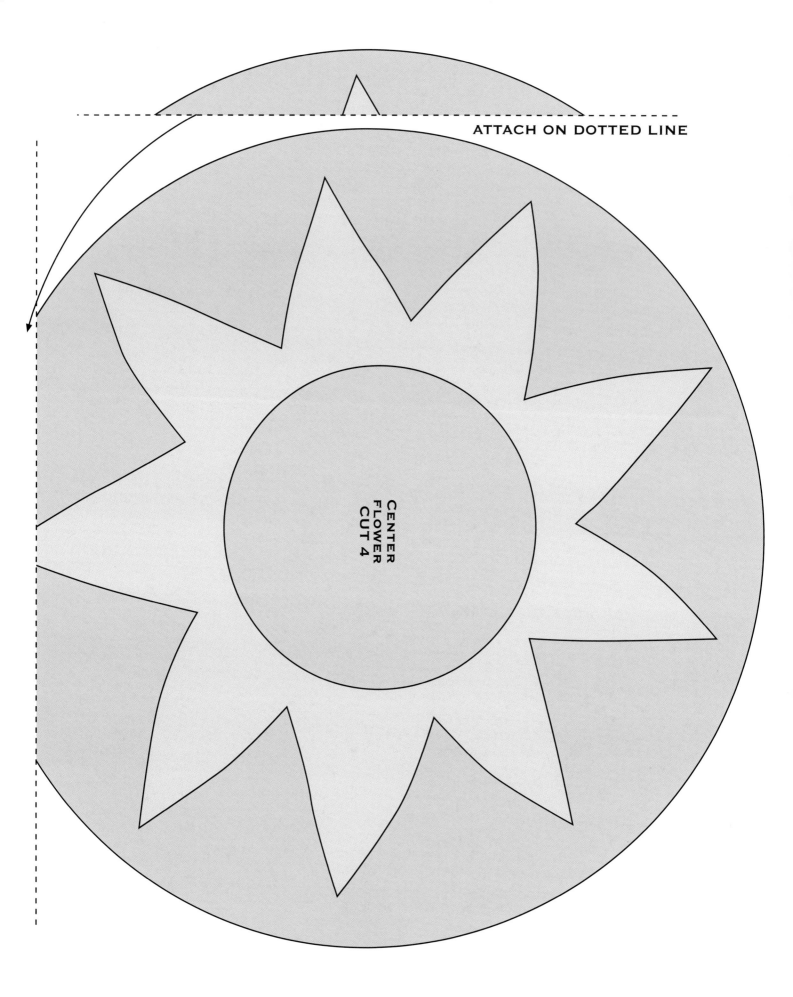

ATTACH ON DOTTED LINE

CENTER
FLOWER
CUT 4

(Plant in) Straight Rows

Size: 66" x 78"

Requirements

★ 2 yards fabric for outside border

★ 3/4 yard fabric for inside borders

★ 1 1/4 yards red fabric for strips and binding

★ At least 10 and up to 20 browns for a total of 4 1/2 yards – the browns need to be medium and dark.

Mom's Glads

I tried growing gladiolas because my grandmother always had them on the farm and when they lived in town. Mine always fell over and were never happy where I had them.

I remember being in the car with my parents, brother and sister and holding the birthday cake for my grandmother – it said MOM. I asked my mother how old Mom would be. She figured up and said 51. I thought about this a lot and finally decided I wanted to live to be that OLD because she still had a LOT of fun.

Instructions

★ There are 27 hourglass blocks and 27 four-patch blocks. Refer to the quilt photo as needed for placement.

★ Hourglass blocks: cut 27 squares 8 1/2". Place right sides together and draw a diagonal line. Sew 1/4" on both sides of this line. Cut apart on the drawn line. Press.

★ Put one of these together with a pair of other prints, matching the center seam. And draw a diagonal line down the center and sew 1/4" on each side of line. Cut apart and press.

★ Square up the block to 7" (this includes the seam allowance). When squaring up, make sure to put the square ruler markings on the sewn diagonal line and the center at 3 1/2". Cut 2 sides and turn the block, line up the ruler the same way and cut at 7". Perfect.

★ Four-patch blocks: Cut strips 4" x width of fabric of brown for the four-patch. Sew 2 strips together. Cut apart at 4" and sew to a strip made of 2 different browns.

★ Sew alternating blocks into 6 rows of 9 blocks.

★ Borders: The inside border between the rows and at the top, bottom, and sides is 1 3/4" wide. Cut the outside border 6" wide.

Easy Stars

Size: 78" x 92"   Linda designed this pattern in 1994.

Requirements

- ★ 1/2 yard each of 13 light fabrics
- ★ 1/2 yard each of 13 mediums and dark fabrics
- ★ 3/4 yard for Border 1
- ★ 3/4 yard for Border 3
- ★ 1 1/2 yards for Border 4
- ★ 1/2 yard for binding

Character

As the years pass, we grow into our character. I have always said wrinkles and laugh lines add character to our face. When we are young, our faces are a blank map.

When I was shopping at a large department store, I looked in a mirror about a football field away and wondered what my grandmother was doing there. I turned to look - it was me. I always loved my grandmother very much and all the wonderful character lines in her face. I treasure mine since I look exactly like her. The only way to avoid wrinkles is to keep your skin "puffed out." This is also called maintaining a healthy weight. You will notice real thin people always look older than their years (and not as happy). I intend to 'puff out' my wrinkles.

Instructions

★ Cut out a total of 49 blocks. Each star uses 2 fabrics. Each heart uses 8 fabrics. I used 3 hearts and 46 stars.

Stars

★ Background fabrics are E, H, F, I and K.

★ Star fabrics are A, B, C, D, G and J.

★ A, B and C may be cut as 1 piece, particularly if you are using a calico or large print. When using stripes, plaids or large checks, I like the direction changes of 3 separate pieces.

Piecing sequence

★ Unit 1: sew together A, B, and C.

★ Unit 2: sew together D and E.

★ Unit 3: sew together F, G, and H.

★ Unit 4: sew together I, J, and K.

★ Sew Unit 2 to Unit 1, add Unit 3, then 4 with 1 thread.

Hearts

★ Piece together 4 background pieces and the 4 heart pieces. They are 4" x 5" (plus seam allowance). Then cut the heart out of the one four-pieced block. Align the center mark on the heart and appliqué in place. Trim out excess fabric behind the heart.

★ Sew the stars together in 7 horizontal rows of 7 each, adding the 3 hearts as shown in the quilt photo. Sew the rows together.

Borders

★ Border 1 is cut 2 1/2" wide.

★ Border 2: Cut varying strips 1 1/2" x 2" plus seam allowance (+sa) of all remaining fabrics except the 2 border fabrics (1 & 3). Sew these strips together in groups of 5 or 6 on the long side. Cut these strips 4" (+sa) and sew together again into very long strips.

★ Border 3 is cut 1 1/2" wide.

★ Border 4 is cut 6 1/2" wide.

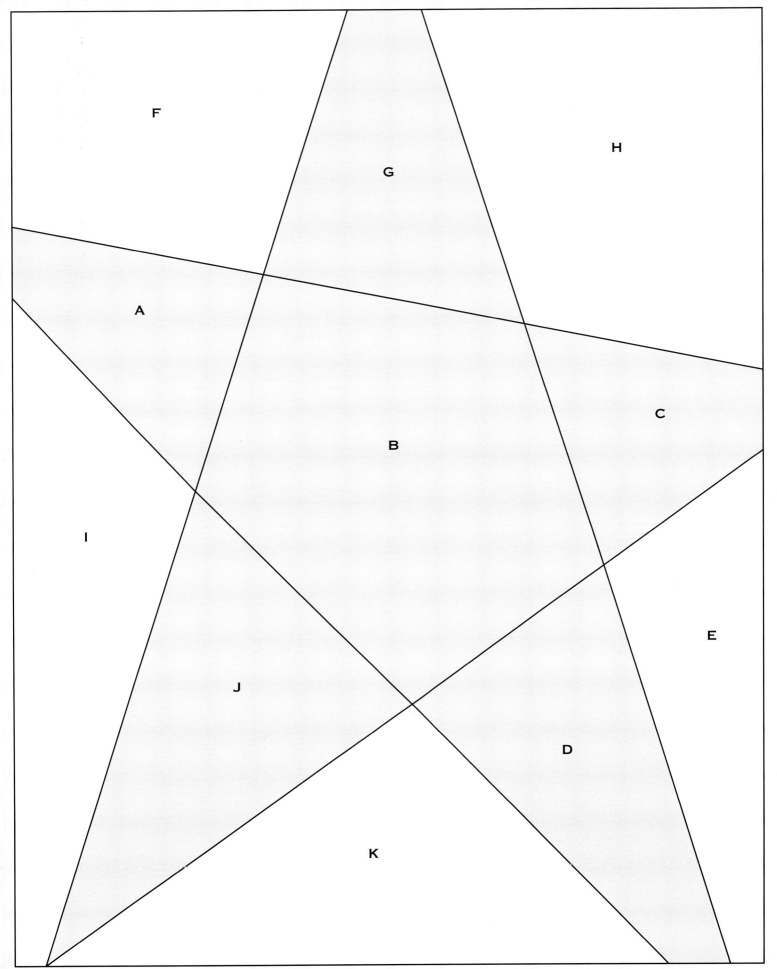

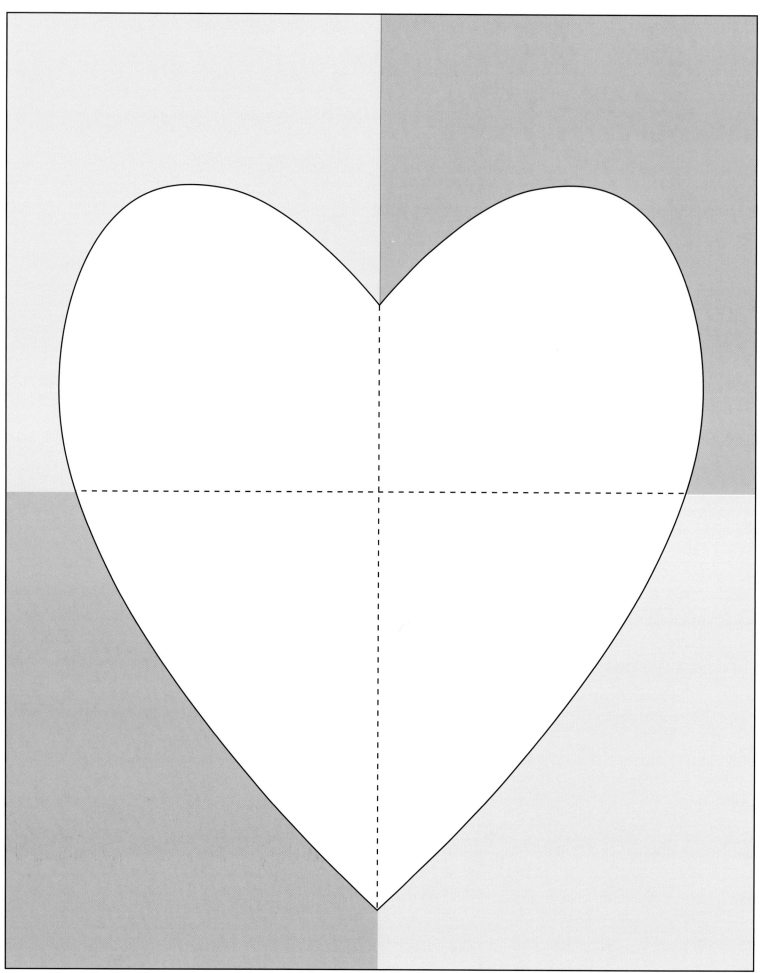

Lady's Garden Club and Sewing Circle

Size: 41" x 61 1/2"

Musings

Does quilting remain as exciting when you age, like in your 60s and 70s? I had a hint yesterday that it does. An "elderly" lady in a wheelchair was buying backing for two twin-size quilts for her twin great-granddaughters. She was excited about quilting these and starting more. There are always family and friends wanting your quilts and what a joy to give them and see them used. The more they are used and loved, the more mellow their colors become - what we try to achieve by dyeing in the first place.

Fern leaf tansy planted by the door keeps ants out.

Paint your porch ceiling blue, it fools the birds and bees into thinking it is the sky and they won't build nests there.

Nobody can make you feel inferior without your consent.
—Eleanor Roosevelt

One never notices what has been done; one can only see what remains to be done.
—Marie Curie

Requirements

- ★ 1/4 yard each of red, pumpkin, brown, blue and green fabric for dresses
- ★ 1/8 yard brown fabric for basket
- ★ 1/8 yard black fabric for shoes and basket void
- ★ 1/8 yard light fabric for face
- ★ Scrap brown fabric for hair
- ★ Scraps of 2 straw color fabrics for hats
- ★ 1/8 yard each of red, pink and red/orange fabric for hollyhocks
- ★ 1/4 yard each of three green fabrics for stems and leaves
- ★ 1/4 yard of a green/brown print fabric for hollyhock buds

Backgrounds

- ★ 1 yard for 1 fabric to include border
- ★ 1/3 yard of 5 backgrounds for behind Miss Jump
- ★ Scrap of 5-8 more lights for alternate pieced blocks

Instructions

- ★ Cut 5 light backgrounds for Miss Jump 10 1/2" x 17 1/2".
- ★ Cut 5 dresses for Miss Jump (her hands are cut as part of the dress).
- ★ Cut out 5 baskets, 5 handles and 5 black oval voids. Appliqué the voids onto the baskets. Cut out 5 faces, 5 hair, 5 two-piece hats, and 10 black shoes.
- ★ Position the dress on the background and tuck

the shoes under. Appliqué the two hat pieces together. Position the head over the hair and add the hat, then appliqué in place as 1 unit. Tuck the neck under the neckline of the dress. Don't make her neck too short.

- ★ Position the basket with the handle going over her left hand, appliqué in place.
- ★ Cut out 48 - 3 1/2" x 4 1/2" rectangles of light fabrics. Sew together in 3 vertical rows of 4. These are the alternate pieced blocks.
- ★ Refer to the photo for placement and sew the 5 club ladies with the alternate blocks in 3 rows. Sew on 4 1/2" borders.

Hollyhocks

- ★ Adding these from the left side, you need:
- ★ #1 left side - 52" stem, 6 buds, 10 flowers, 3 leaves
- ★ #2 - 44" stem, 6 buds, 7 flowers, 3 leaves
- ★ #3 - 53" stem, 4 buds, 2 small flowers, 3 buds, 8 flowers, 3 leaves
- ★ #4 - 16" stem, 4 buds, 4 flowers, 1 leaf
- ★ #5 - 17" stem, 2 buds, 3 flowers, 3 leaves
- ★ By varying the flower seam allowances (1/4" or 1/8"), you will get more variation in the flower and bud sizes.
- ★ The finished width of the stems are 3/4" to 1 1/8". Appliqué them in place, referring to the photo.

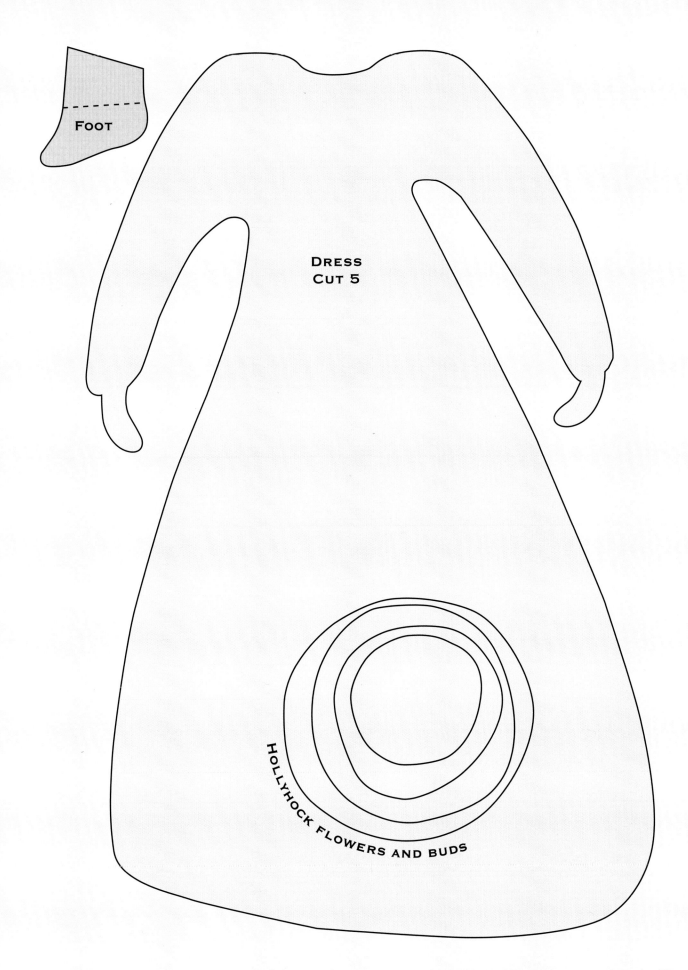

FOOT

DRESS
CUT 5

HOLLYHOCK FLOWERS AND BUDS

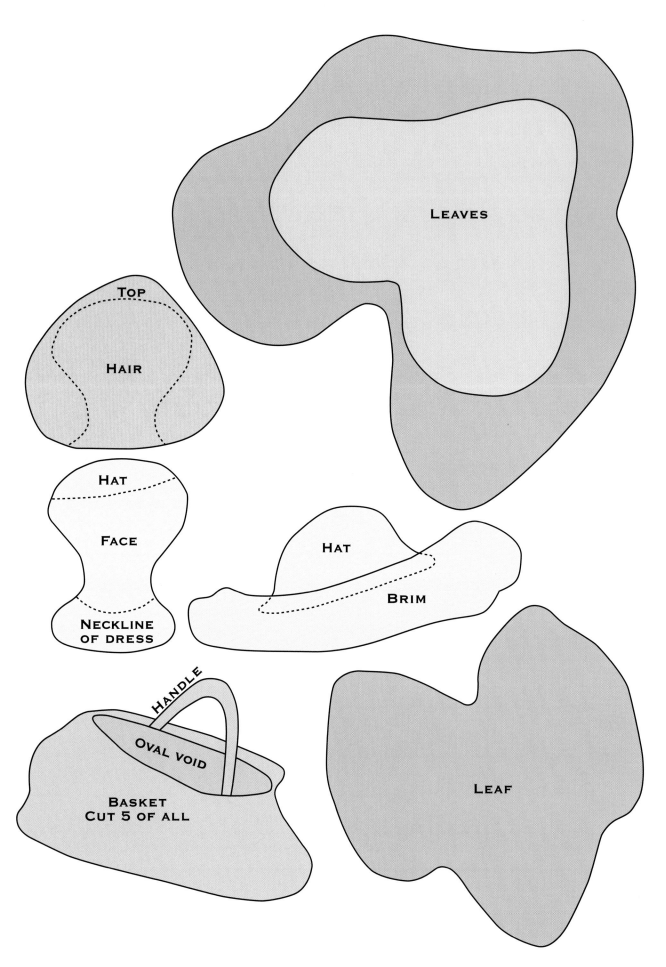

LEAVES

TOP

HAIR

HAT

FACE

NECKLINE
OF DRESS

HAT

BRIM

HANDLE

OVAL VOID

BASKET
CUT 5 OF ALL

LEAF

The Gardener

Size: 44" x 44"

My Garden...

is now overflowing. All the pink hollyhocks are blooming. Some are 8' tall. One is really different, it has the outside row of petals, then skips about 12" and has many short petals about 1/2" long. It looks like a poodle cut. I have seen double hollyhocks before but I don't know what this one is. We had a bird bath in the flowers and in hot weather, the birds had to line up to take their baths, sometimes three birds would bathe at once. I have seen a total of seven baby birds bathing at once and the mother on the sidelines teaching them. I'm sure she must run a day care. I don't think sparrows have seven babies in one nest. Anyway, I decided to get another birdbath but we dropped the top and cracked it. I have an old cat birdbath - a cat lying down, the back part is the birdbath. The birds didn't bathe in it much because it was on the ground. After putting it on a pedestal (using the screw top of a canning jar between), the birds are using it and it is my favorite one.

We have red birds, robins, purple and yellow finches, a mockingbird, brown thrush, small woodpeckers, house wrens, sparrows, blue jays and purple martins.

Requirements

★ 1/4 yard each of 3 backgrounds

★ 1/8 yard for heads (with enough contrast to show on background)

★ 2 yards green print for background

★ 1/2 yard lighter green print for vines and leaves

★ 1/4 yard navy for 2 dresses

★ 1/4 yard brown for 2 dresses

★ 1/4 yard red for 1 dress

★ Scraps of straw and gold colors for hats

★ 1/8 yard each of reds, yellows and blues for flower blossoms and centers

★ 1 yard red for outside border and binding

Instructions

★ Cut 5 gardeners with heads and hats. Mark the top of the sleeves.

Piecing Sequence

★ Fold template A in half (opposite corners together) and press to position head on center line, refer to photo if necessary. Appliqué head (template B). Add dress bodice (template C).

★ Sew background (templates D and F) to each side of dress sleeve (template F). The top of sleeve will meet dress bodice (template G). Add dress bodice to sleeve unit and add background (template H). Refer to illustration #1 on page 43. Repeat, reversing the templates.

★ Sew background (template I and Ir) to sides of skirt (template J) and add to dress bodice (template K) at top.

★ Sew sections together, referring to ilustration #1.

★ Fold a 1/4" tuck in the brim of hat and appliqué tuck down. Position the hat over the edge of the tuck and appliqué them together, then onto

gardener's head, keeping fairly straight as to keep sun off her face.

Green Borders

★ Cut 4 triangles (#1) and 4 triangles (#2) from green fabric adding allowances. Measurements include seam allowance.

★ Cut 4 strips from selvage to selvage 3 1/2" wide. From these strips, cut:

2 strips 18 1/2" (#3),

2 strips 48 1/2" (#4) and

8 strips 12 1/2" (#5).

★ Refer to Assembly diagram to stitch these together.

Vine

★ Cut 8 vines from light green fabric. Position one in each corner and the rest to connect the corner vines. You will need to trim some ends. Cut 4 stems (template 16) used near the center gardener. Cut 4 stems (template 15) used with some tulips. Cut 8 stems (template 17) for remaining flowers. Cut a total of 50 leaves, referring to the templates for amount of each. You can use more leaves if you like. Cut 25 flowers, referring to the templates for the amount of each.

Red Outside Borders

★ The following measurements include seam allowances:

★ Cut 2 strips - 4" x 43" and add to the top and bottom of the quilt.

★ Cut 2 strips - 4"x 50" and add to the sides of the quilt. Add batting and backing.

ASSEMBLY DIAGRAM

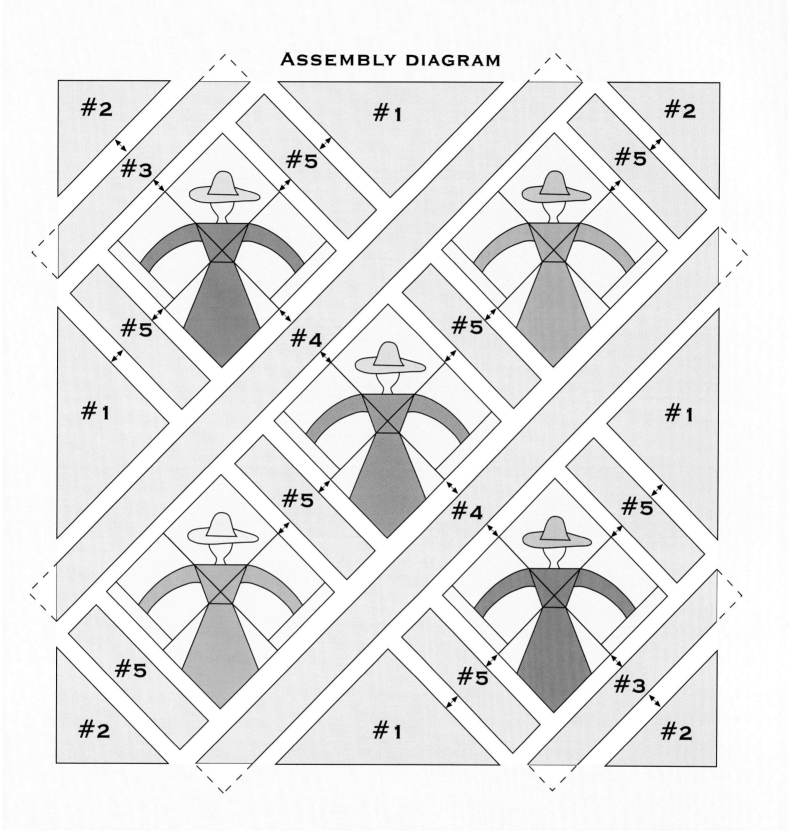

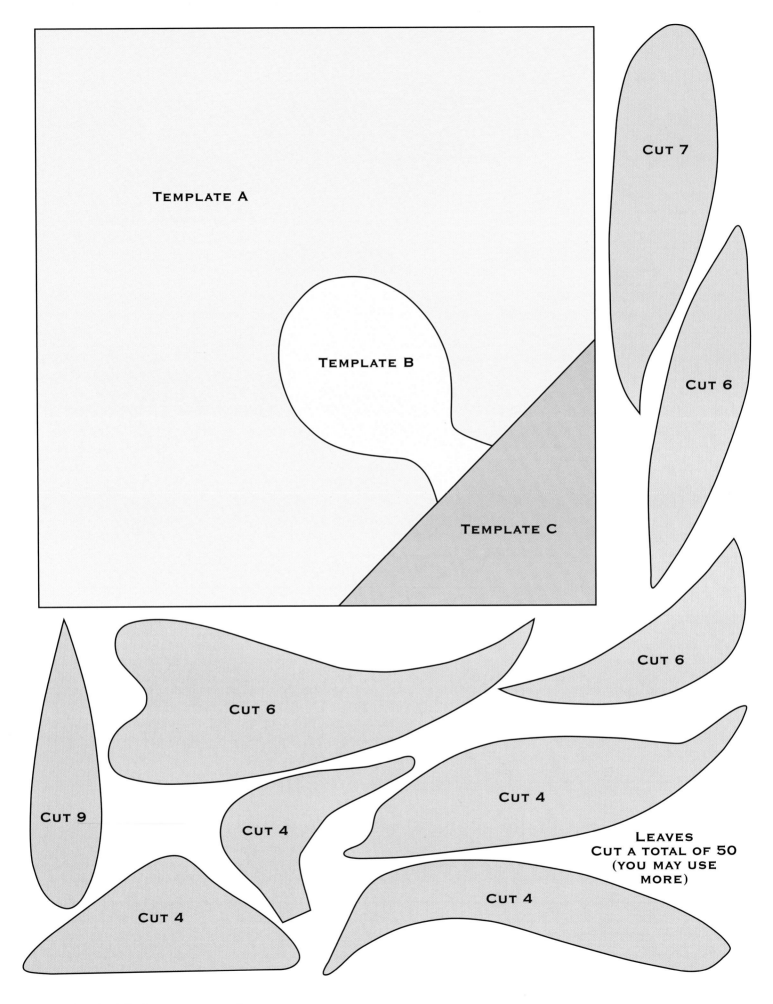

TEMPLATE A

TEMPLATE B

TEMPLATE C

CUT 7

CUT 6

CUT 6

CUT 6

CUT 9

CUT 4

CUT 4

CUT 4

CUT 4

LEAVES
CUT A TOTAL OF 50
(YOU MAY USE
MORE)

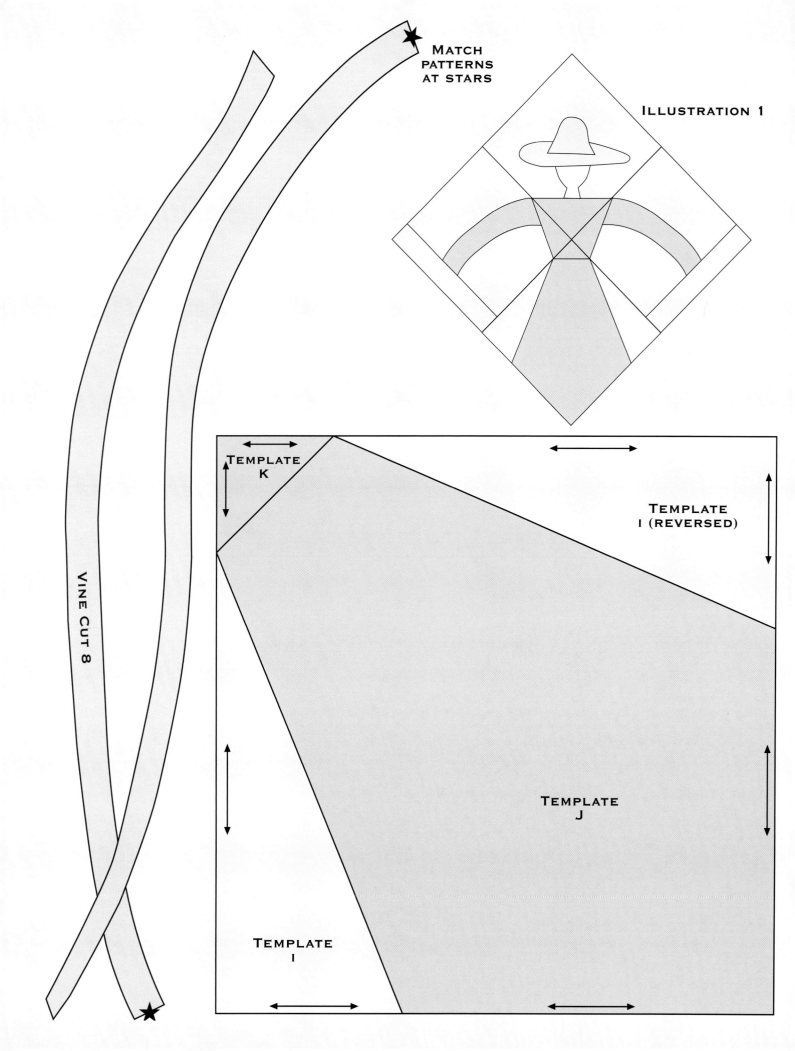

MATCH
PATTERNS
AT STARS

ILLUSTRATION 1

VINE CUT 8

TEMPLATE
K

TEMPLATE
I (REVERSED)

TEMPLATE
J

TEMPLATE
I

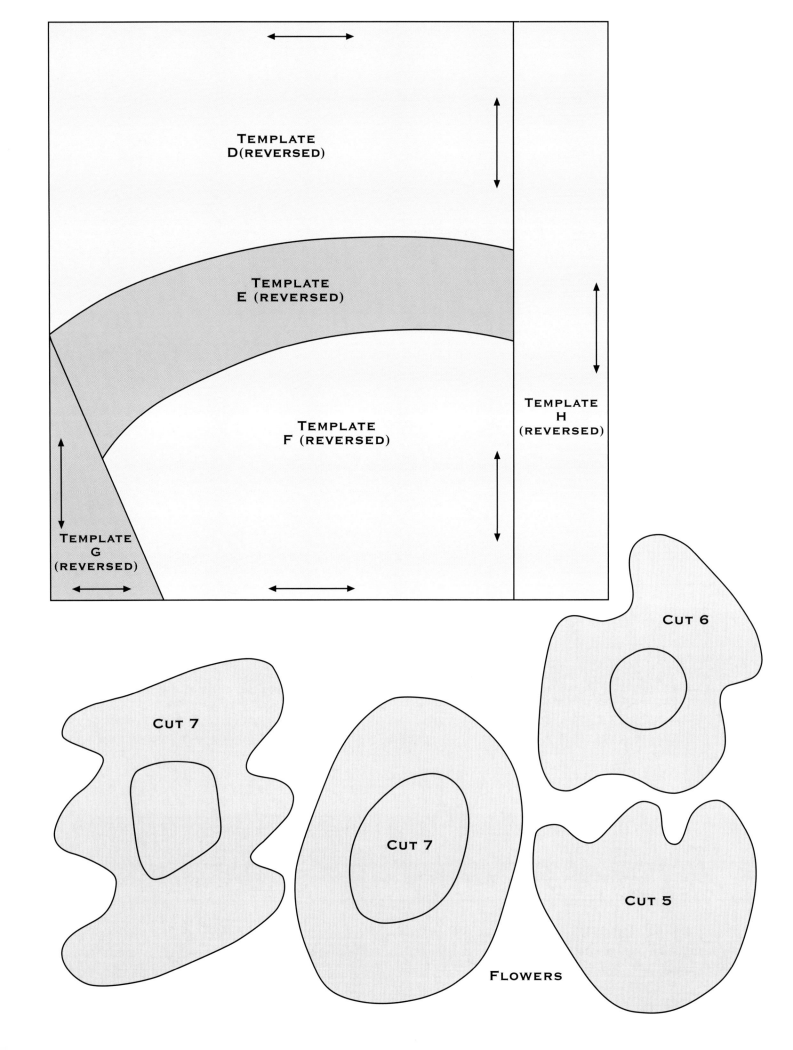

TEMPLATE
D(REVERSED)

TEMPLATE
E (REVERSED)

TEMPLATE
F (REVERSED)

TEMPLATE
G
(REVERSED)

TEMPLATE
H
(REVERSED)

CUT 6

CUT 7

CUT 7

CUT 5

FLOWERS

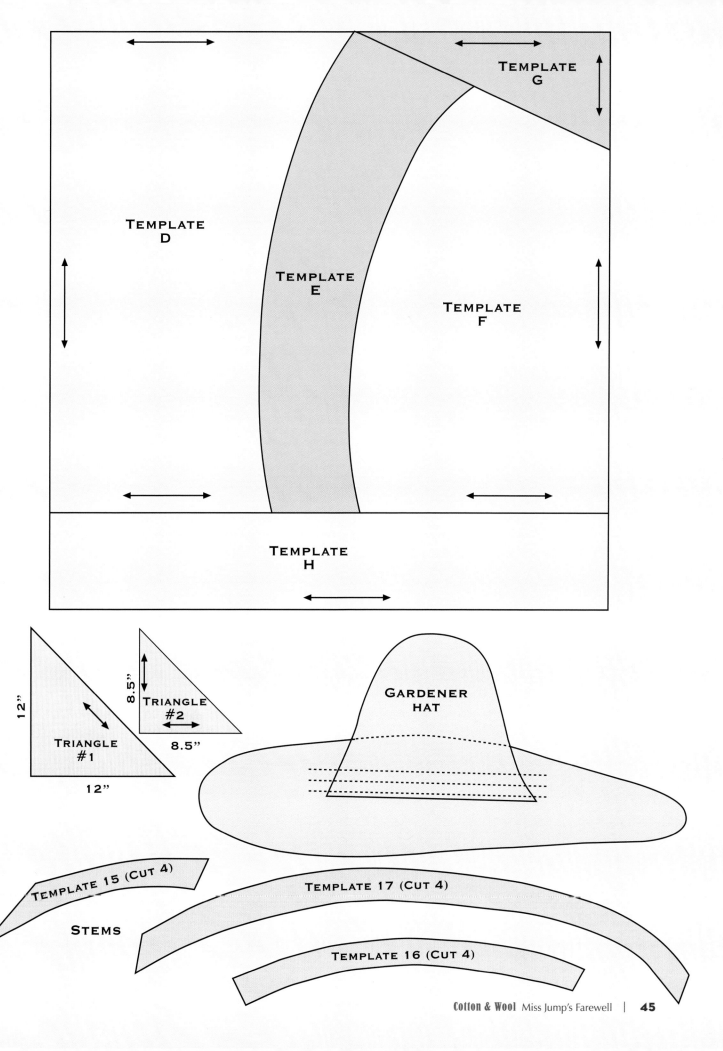

TEMPLATE
D

TEMPLATE
E

TEMPLATE
G

TEMPLATE
F

TEMPLATE
H

TRIANGLE
#1

TRIANGLE
#2

12"

12"

8.5"

8.5"

GARDENER
HAT

STEMS

TEMPLATE 15 (CUT 4)

TEMPLATE 17 (CUT 4)

TEMPLATE 16 (CUT 4)

Projects

Memory Box and Needlecase

Box size: 7" x 18" (or 20")

Use yours for keeping treasures, sewing supplies, keys, postcards, favorite snapshots, etc. I like to keep special photos in my memory box. Sometimes the photos are of the garden, lots of the time the photos are of our dog, Sugar, and our grandchildren.

Childhood

My playhouse was sticks and string.

The space between my house and the neighbors was only about 8', with an 18' high retaining wall down the center. How perfect. This was the kitchen counter and cook surface. I stacked sticks in the ground to designate the doorways, then stretched string for the walls. I know I had a living room, kitchen and bedroom for the dolls.

Near the wall, away from the house, grew an abundance of bushes that produced red berries. They were perfect for picking, squashing and feeding to my dolls. I'm sure during my eighth and ninth year, the birds wondered what happened to their berries. I spent many happy hours between the houses playing dolls. It was shady and not much grew there anyway.

Materials Needed

- ★ 1/2" pine wood
- ★ Wool – 22" x 22" for background and needlecase

  6" x 18" piece for inside of box

  6" x 18" piece for outside of box

  5" x 5" scrap for star
- ★ Scraps of heavy cotton for 2 hearts
- ★ 18" medium rickrack for needlecase
- ★ 1 mother of pearl button or other small button
- ★ Scrap of felt to save needles in
- ★ One skein black wool thread
- ★ Pearl grey embroidery thread for heart on needlecase

Constructing the box

- ★ Get out your saw and wood glue or have your favorite woodworker make this box. Cut out the pattern pieces on pages xx and xx. Assemble the box in the way you prefer (glue, nail). Sand lightly if needed and it's ready to cover.

How to Cover the Box

- ★ Lay the box back pattern (pages xx and xx) on the largest piece of wool and cut 2. Add a 1/4" seam on all sides. Sew the wool together around the box back with a buttonhole stitch. Start stitching on one side of the box, go up the side, around the top, down the other side…continue until you reach the starting point.
- ★ Cut one 15" x 4 3/4" for the outside of box and one the same size for the inside of the box.

- ★ Cut one 6 1/2"" x 4 1/2" piece of wool for the bottom front of the box. Sew the star onto the wool before stitching the rest of the cover on the box. Cut a piece of cardboard 5 3/8" x 3".
- ★ Using glue or double sided tape, cover the cardboard and slip it into the bottom of the box.
- ★ This holds the wool down inside the box. Now decorate the box with your favorite things or sewing supplies. I put 2 eye screws on the back about 2" apart and a piece of wire between them so I could hang this up. Have fun. I love this box.

Needlecase Instructions

- ★ Cut a rectangle of wool 6" x 4 1/2".
- ★ Cut a rectangle of felt 5" x 3 3/4".
- ★ Cut a closure of wool 5/8" x 4 1/4".
- ★ Sew this closure on the backside of the needlecase at the center point (see Needlecase diagram). I used one strand of regular cotton thread and small overcast stitches. This is much easier and faster than you think.
- ★ Sew the rickrack on, catching each side so it stays flat (see Rickrack diagram).
- ★ Center the felt on the wool and sew from top to bottom.
- ★ The buttonhole is hand stitched, the same way as the tab is attached. Sew on the button. I added a cross-stitched heart to the front of my needlecase.

Tip

- ★ When I find a wooden object I want to recreate, I make a model of it using cardboard. Then my husband knows the exact dimensions to use for the final project.

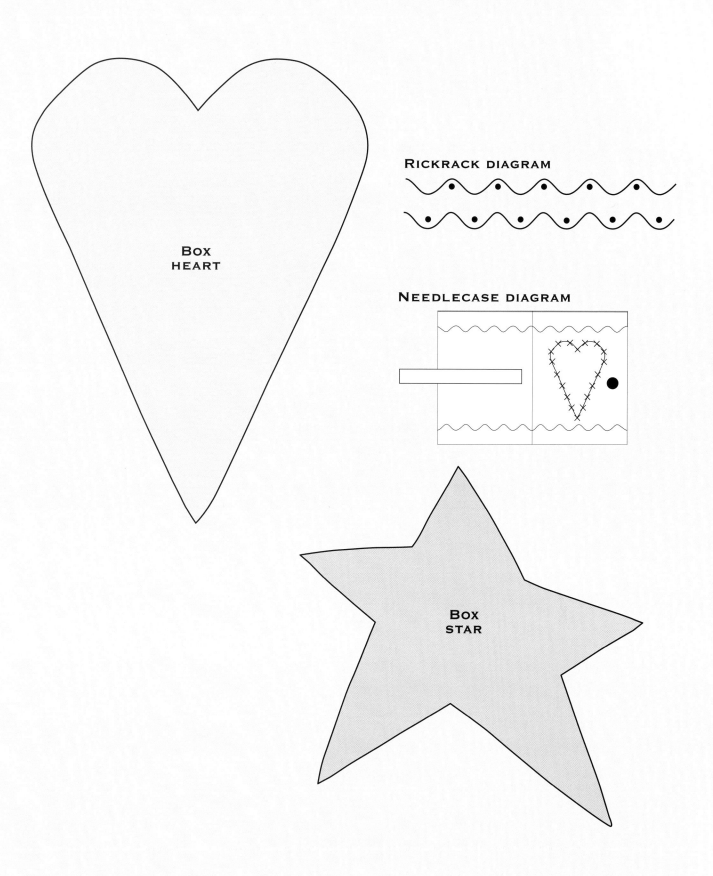

BOX
HEART

RICKRACK DIAGRAM

NEEDLECASE DIAGRAM

BOX
STAR

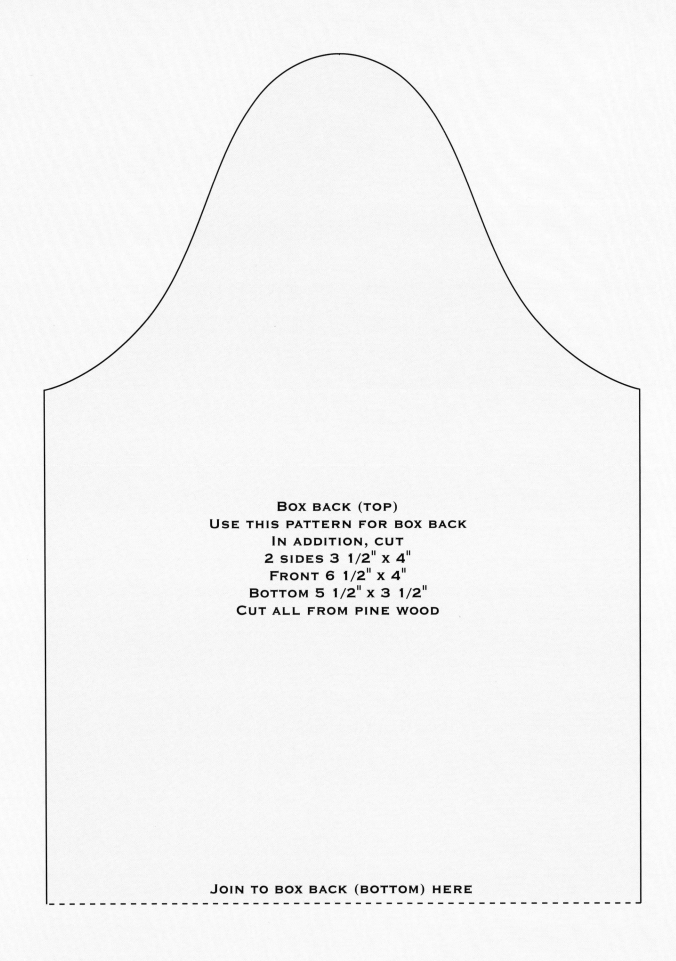

BOX BACK (TOP)
USE THIS PATTERN FOR BOX BACK
IN ADDITION, CUT
2 SIDES 3 1/2" x 4"
FRONT 6 1/2" x 4"
BOTTOM 5 1/2" x 3 1/2"
CUT ALL FROM PINE WOOD

JOIN TO BOX BACK (BOTTOM) HERE

JOIN TO BOX BACK (TOP) HERE

BOX BACK
(BOTTOM)

NOTE: ADD 2" TO THIS END FOR TALLER VERSION

Feedsack Apron

Truly "one size fits all"

History: When husband Bob retired, he started baking bread and making a flour mess. He wears this apron for all baking and cooking. I have noticed he never leaves the house in it—except when he is making the most wonderful pizza dough and he needs basil from the garden.

Fabrics

I have loved fabrics since I can remember. I can remember sitting under a weeping willow tree in the back yard with fabric remnants figuring out what to make for my dolls. Remember when summer was so very long. By the time I was 12, I was always after the feedsacks at my grandparents farm. One sack made a pair of shorts for me or if we were lucky enough to have two sacks matching, I could have a skirt. And I used zippers, but had to walk a street over and a block down to a ladies home that sewed a buttonhole for the waistband for 5 cents.

Materials Needed

★ One large feedsack per apron (19" x 39 1/2") I used one that is seamless (these bags were like circles with a seam stitched to close the bottom—no other seams). The ones I used say FULTON SEAMLESS around a circle with an A in it and under that the words extra heavy.

★ Cotton rug hooking tape

★ Off-white cotton thread

Instructions

★ Turn the feedsack wrong side out—wash and dry it. Remove the bottom seam of the feedsack. Measure between the feedsack's woven lines to find the center back. Mark from top to bottom and cut it open on this line. I like all the printed area on the center front and right side up.

★ Cut armhole openings referring to the diagram. I cut one, then fold the apron in half and the other armhole the same. Shorter people need a shallower armhole cut than taller people.

★ Hold the apron up against yourself and check the bib width. This can be made narrower by cutting wider armholes. Remember, it will be finished with a 3/4" seam. Turn under 1/4" and then another 1/2" edge from the heart (on diagram) around all sides, except for the lower edge. I like mine let fringed—it is up to you.

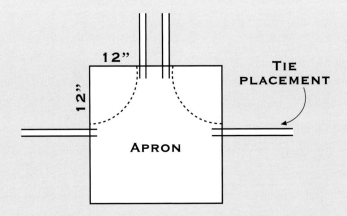

★ Cut a 52" tie from the rug hooking tape and stitch it on each side of apron and knot the other end. My neck tie length is 25 1/2". Pin yours to the apron and try it on. Make sure it is comfortable. You could be spending a lot of time with this around your neck.

★ Bob doesn't want a pocket in his. He tucks a kitchen towel into the belt as it comes around to tie in the front, just like a baker.

Bedside Caddy
Size: 19" x 26"

A bedside table is fine but if you leave things on it, it does look messy. The Bedside Caddy is made to keep essentials at hand in bed or on the arm of an upholstered chair. It is designed to slip between the mattress and box springs on the bed or over the arm and beneath the seat cushion on an upholstered chair. I use mine to hold the television remote control, tissues and cough drops.

Two of my superstitions

I never give away a quilt or wallhanging without sleeping under it first. I have always felt this is bad luck. When sleeping under it, I try to fill it with good wishes.

I don't have candles displayed in the house without burning their wicks. Unused wicks makes the candle look like it is never used.

Materials Needed

★ 3/4 yard fabric for outside

★ 3/4 yard coordinating fabric for inside

★ 1/4 yard fabric for trim

★ 1 1/4 yard large rickrack for trim (dyed)

★ 1 yard medium rickrack (dyed)

★ 5 large buttons (old or new)

★ 1 yard fusible or plain fleece batting

Instructions

★ Cut caddy front and back fabric 20" x 36". Lay this fabric on top of the batting and cut the batting the same size. If fusible batting is used, press it onto wrong side of the front or back, according to the instructions on the batting package.

★ Cut the binding 2 1/2" wide (you may want to piece it if you use a plaid, stripe, or check and want it on the bias which looks great). Press the strip in half lengthwise to add to the top layer of the caddy only.

★ Cut the trim piece 2 1/2" wide (you may want to piece it if you use a plaid, stripe or check and want it on the bias, which looks great). Position this strip on the bottom edge - remember this will be turned up - so you might call this the wrong side. Tuck the large rickrack under the binding. The side rickrack pieces go in when you sew the side seams.

★ Arrange these layers: the big back (right side up), caddy front (right side down), caddy back, then the batting. Stitch around the top and both side edges. Trim the corners, turn it right side out and press.

★ Mark 10" from the bottom edge. Fold up this edge to make the caddy pocket. Before sewing it in place along the edges, arrange all of your trims and buttons. Place the large rickrack along the pocket edge, then between the side seams. Pin and stitch all this in place. The smaller rickrack is sewn to make the pocket divisions—stitch these into the sizes to hold the objects you desire.

★ Slide the top 10" to 15" of the caddy between the bed mattress and box springs at the side where it is most convenient. Follow the photo to arrange yours.

Star Placemats
Size: 21 1/2" x 15 1/2"

History: I wanted some Christmas placemats that made a statement – especially by themselves. These do not have to be for Christmas and do not have to be red and green.

Materials Needed

★ Cotton twill fabric - 2/3 yard of 3 different stripes will make 3 placemats

★ Wool for each star 18" x 16"

★ Cotton thread to match wool

★ Tan cotton thread for assembly and quilting

★ Fleece batting

Instructions

★ Cut out the wool star in 1 piece. It is easiest to make a freezer paper pattern and press it onto the right side of the wool with the shiny side of freezer paper down. Do not leave a seam allowance.

★ Cut background twill fabric 18" x 14 1/2" (all the measurements include the seam allowance).

★ Cut 2 side borders 2 1/2" x 18".

★ Cut 1 bottom border 2 1/2" x 24".

★ Sew the borders onto the background and miter the 2 bottom corners.

★ Position the wool star on the background and let 1 5/8" extend over the top. The star is stitched onto the background with a machine buttonhole stitch in matching thread.

★ Cut a piece of batting the size of your placemat.

★ Arrange the layers like this: back, right side up; front, right side down, and then the fleece batting.

★ Pin the sides and bottom, then turn over to sew. *If you sew with the fleece side up, it will catch on your presser foot.*

★ Trim the corners, turn right side out and press. Turn under the front and back top edges of the placemat and hand whipstitch to close.

★ Quilting suggestion: Outline the border and the star and the 5 lines inside the star.

JOIN TO
TOP OF
STAR

JOIN TO RIGHT OF STAR

STAR PLACEMAT

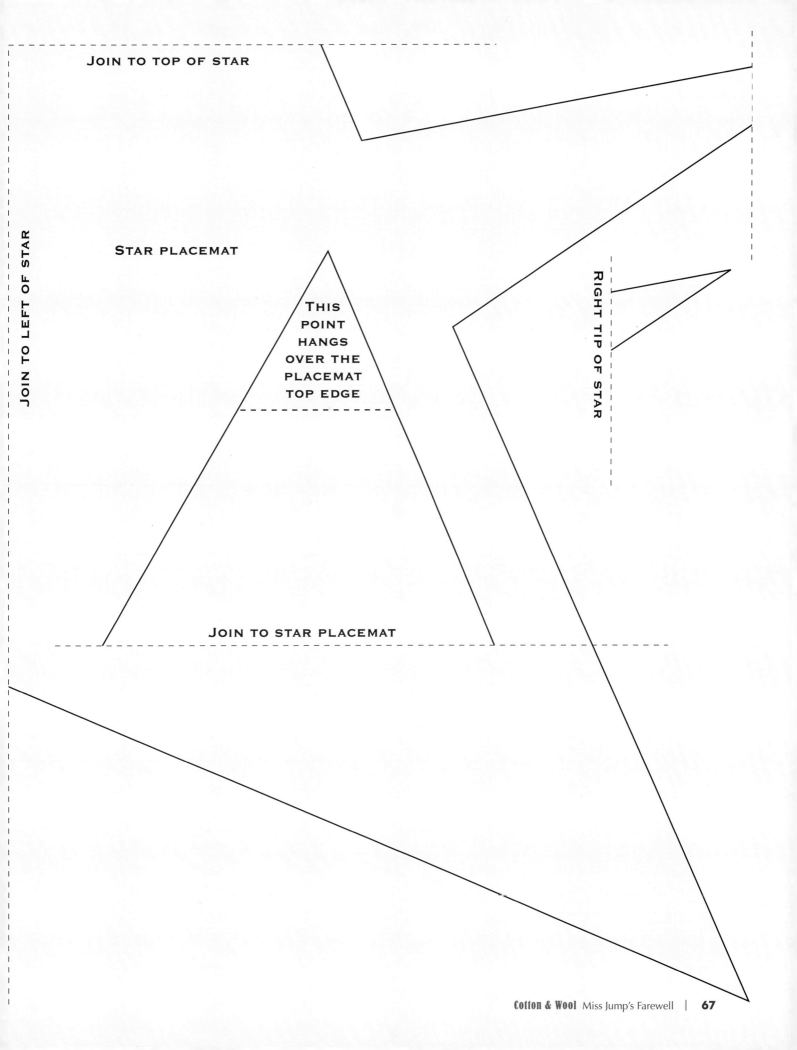

JOIN TO TOP OF STAR

JOIN TO LEFT OF STAR

STAR PLACEMAT

RIGHT TIP OF STAR

THIS POINT HANGS OVER THE PLACEMAT TOP EDGE

JOIN TO STAR PLACEMAT

Pineapple Tablerunner
Size: 50 1/2" x 15 1/2"

Some say I am obsessed with stars and hearts, but pineapples are definitely third. I sometimes use this as a pillow cover on the bed.

Pineapples, Zinnias and Cockscomb

I dry zinnias all summer. I dry them whole (no stem) in silica gel (follow the directions on the package, it's very easy). Leave them whole and crop them into potpourri. They will get broken a little but will still look good and remind you of summer. Dry the cockscomb by hanging it upside down. They look best after a few years when the colors mellow and soften. After drying the cockscomb, pick out the seeds (they are on the upper part of the stem near the head) for planting next spring. Cockscomb come in red, cream, pink and gold-yellow color.

Three years ago I found some very small pineapple for very little money. I purchased two. I put cloves in the ridges around the eyes. Use a nail to start the hole for the clove and wear gloves. Set them upright on a rack with a cookie sheet under the rack and place in the oven at the lowest setting for three days and nights. They are wonderful. All my friends want one. The trick is finding the small pineapples. The fruit part was no more than 6" tall. Pick one with a good-looking top.

Materials Needed

* ★ Wool – 1 piece darkest green the exact size of the runner, 50 1/2″ x 15 1/2″. Make sure it is very straight: this means tearing it, then pressing the edge with steam so it isn't stretched.

* ★ 4 yards large rickrack dyed taupe

* ★ 1 yard homespun or brushed cotton for the back (will need to be pieced)

* ★ 18″ x 10″ gold plaid wool for pineapples

* ★ 4 - 10″ x 10″ green wools

* ★ 2 or 3 10″ x 10″ red wools

* ★ 15″ x 15″ khaki color or army blanket

* ★ Matching wool thread (gold) for pineapples

* ★ Matching regular cotton thread for everything else

Instructions

* ★ Wool pieces do not need seam allowances and are not turned back. Cut out 3 gold pineapples, 2 plant stems (1 and 1 reversed), 3 green star tops, 5 red hearts, 4 medium red arcs, and 4 small and 4 large arc of khaki color.

* ★ *Notice I had to stitch green wool leftovers together to make the plant stems.*

* ★ Cut 1 and 1 reversed plant stems, 8 red buds and 2 green buds.

* ★ Appliqué the pineapple with the wool thread using a buttonhole stitch. The rest of the appliqués are sewn with matching cotton thread in the overcast stitch. I like to see the little stitches and this will go much quicker than you think. Position all pieces on background and stitch.

* ★ Cut the backing 3/4″ larger than the runner all the way around and press edges under 3/4″, then layer runner and backing, wrong sides together. Pin the rickrack in place around all edges, stitch.

* ★ It does not need to be quilted, so it is finished. Enjoy.

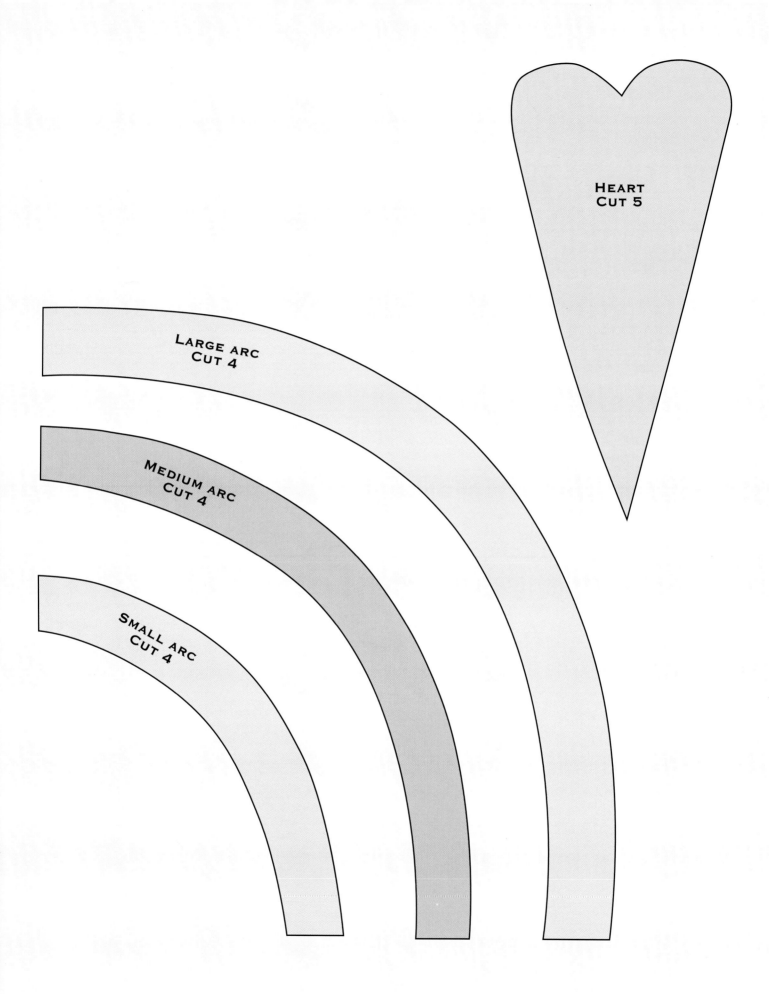

Heart
Cut 5

Large arc
Cut 4

Medium arc
Cut 4

Small arc
Cut 4

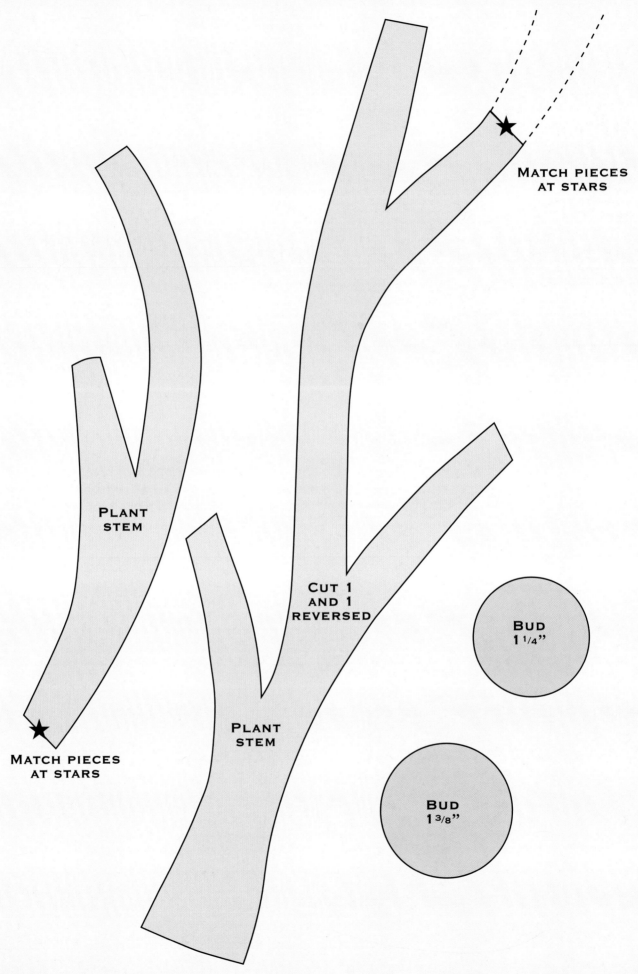

MATCH PIECES
AT STARS

PLANT
STEM

CUT 1
AND 1
REVERSED

BUD
1 ¼"

PLANT
STEM

MATCH PIECES
AT STARS

BUD
1 ³/₈"

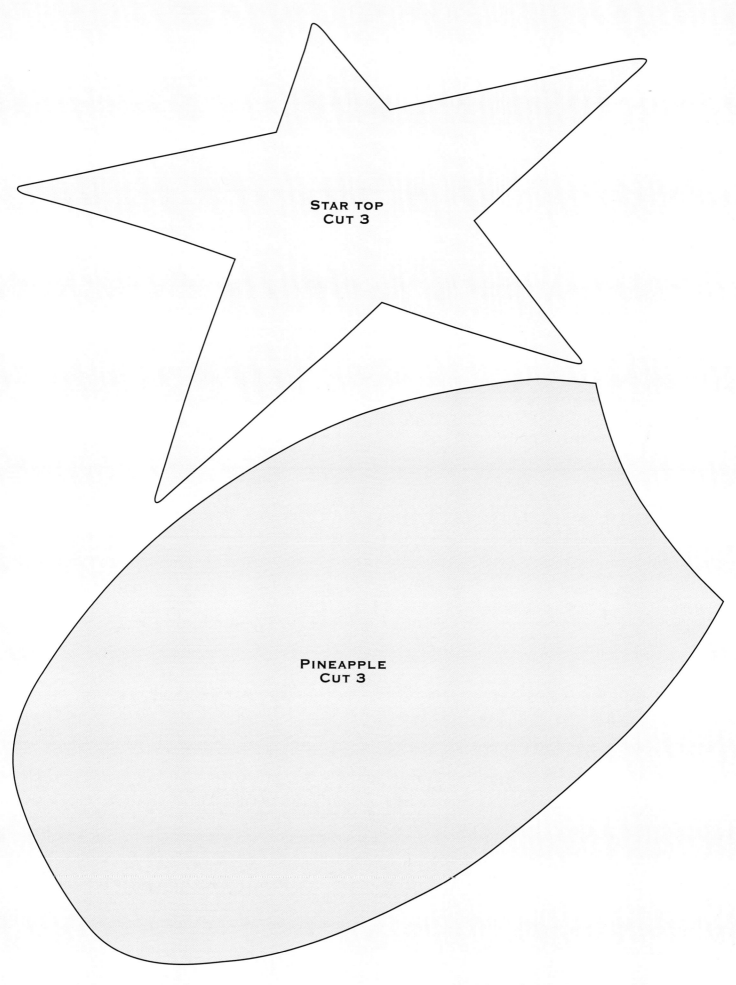

STAR TOP
CUT 3

PINEAPPLE
CUT 3

Angels Tablerunner
Size 63" x 17 1/4"

Yes, I used an old army blanket to make this. I had been collecting these blankets in all the drab olive colors because our son bought a house (sight unseen) in South Dakota and I was going to use them as curtains. Bob (husband), Sugar (little dog) and I got there and counted 49 windows - I knew we had a lot of flea market and antique shopping to do. Sometimes things work out for the best. Sugar did not like traveling or being in South Dakota and after having to find a veterinarian at 2 a.m. on two occasions, we gave up. Yes, Sugar rules. Son has now moved to Minnesota and I have all these great blankets.

Dishcloths, handbags, whatever

My friends from Washington taught me to make a handbag out of two dish towels. Mine was plaid on one side and striped on the other. I immediately started using it.

Sometimes I am very efficient. Very few times, in fact.

This time I packed my things early in the morning for a workshop that evening. Bob lugged everything to the car and then decided to take my car and run some errands.

That afternoon I had an appointment for an MRI of my knees.

Well, my towel handbag was on the top of my sewing things in my car with my keys inside. It didn't help that Bob's car was home—I had no keys. My neighbor drove me to the appointment only a couple miles away and I left a terse note for Bob to pick me up.

I had 45 minutes to calm down in the MRI machine and realized it certainly was not Bob's fault.

I try to think of that often—that 45 minutes saved a lot of hurt feelings.

Materials Needed

★ 1 skein black wool thread for edge

★ Cotton thread to match all other appliqué

★ 6" x 8" wool for moon

★ 8" x 8" wool for dress ruffle

★ 20" x 20" wool for dress and circle under star

★ 15" x 15" white wool for wings, stars, circles

★ 10" x 10" bright red wool for loops at sides

★ Scraps: orange for moon, gold for stars and horns, deep red for hair, arms are slightly lighter than dress, pink for face, at least 4 scraps big enough for stars, brown for boots and inside of horn

★ 65" x 18" background wool

★ 1 yard plaid brushed cotton or homespun for backing

Instructions

★ Tear background wool to 63" x 17 1/4" and steam press so edges are not stretched.

★ I used freezer paper patterns to cut out all pieces of wool. Trace the pattern on the non-shiny side, then roughly cut out and press it (no steam) onto the wool. Cut it out on the lines (do not add a seam allowance), remove the freezer paper and position it on the background wool. I used matching cotton thread and a tiny overcast stitch. You can also use a buttonhole stitch and wool thread.

★ This runner looks great on the back of a sofa, on the dining room table or atop the pillows on the bed. I plan to use it from Thanksgiving eve to Valentine's Day on the guest bed.

★ Attach the backing.

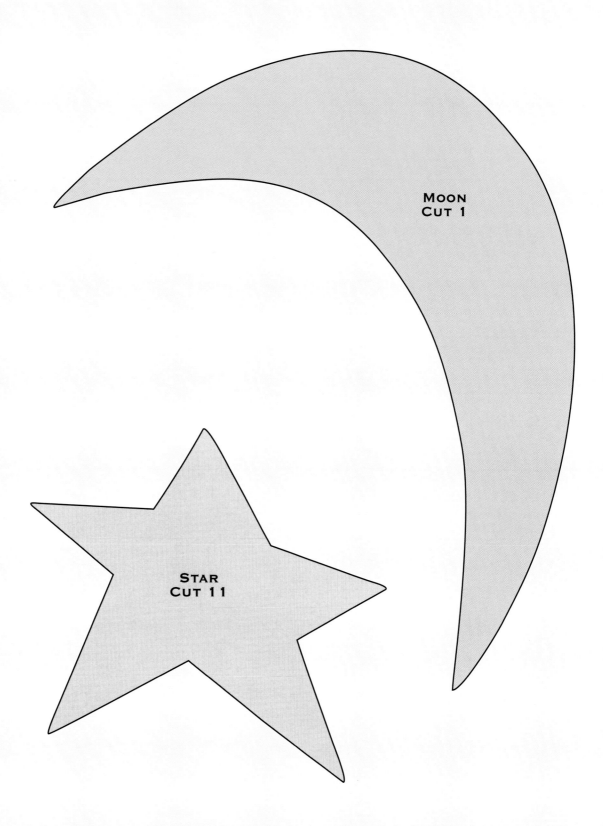

MOON
CUT 1

STAR
CUT 11

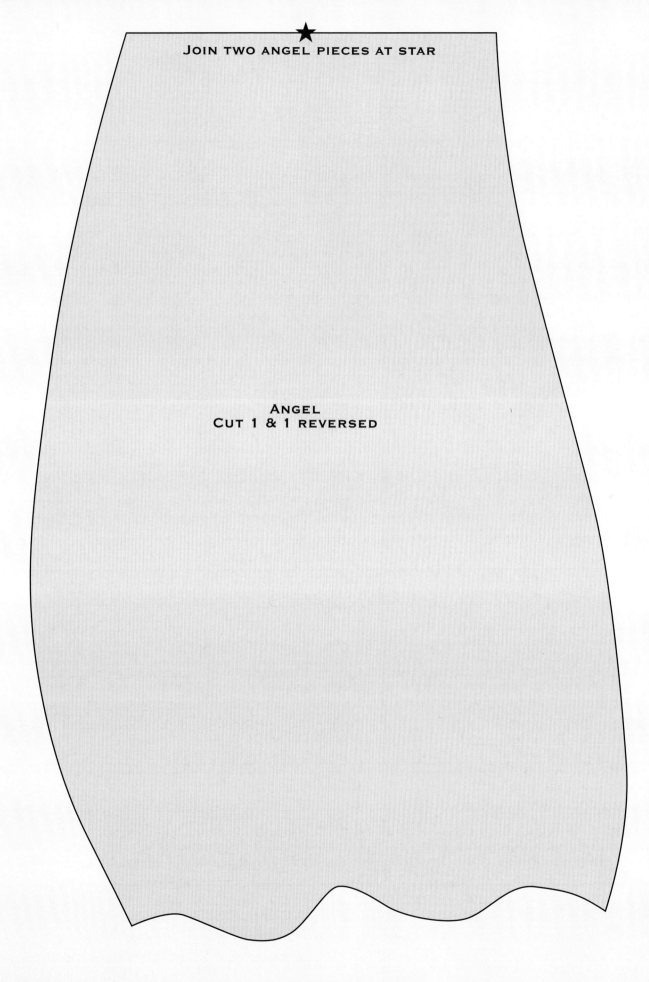

JOIN TWO ANGEL PIECES AT STAR

ANGEL
CUT 1 & 1 REVERSED

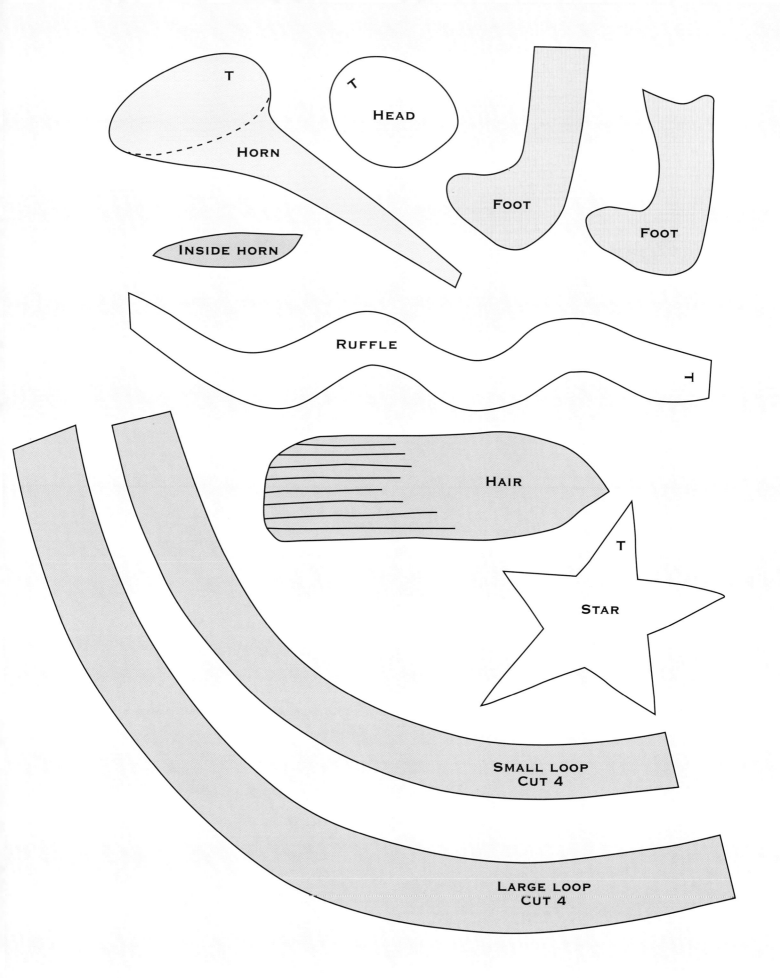

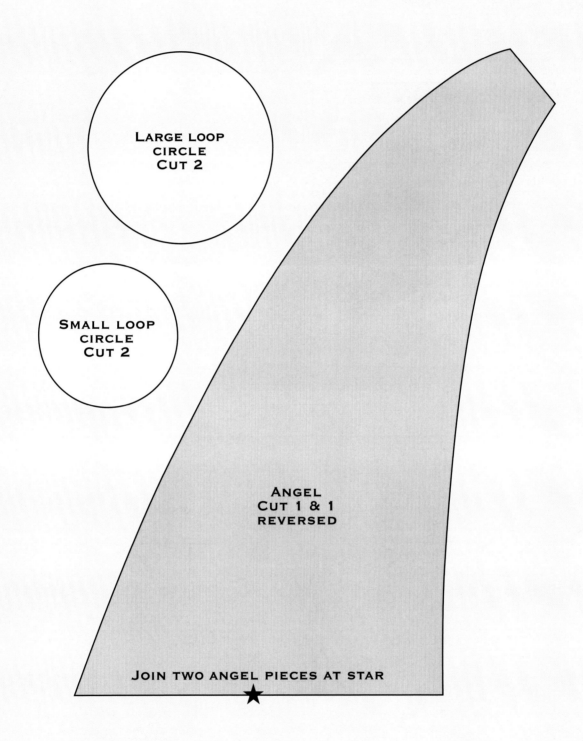

LARGE LOOP
CIRCLE
CUT 2

SMALL LOOP
CIRCLE
CUT 2

ANGEL
CUT 1 & 1
REVERSED

JOIN TWO ANGEL PIECES AT STAR

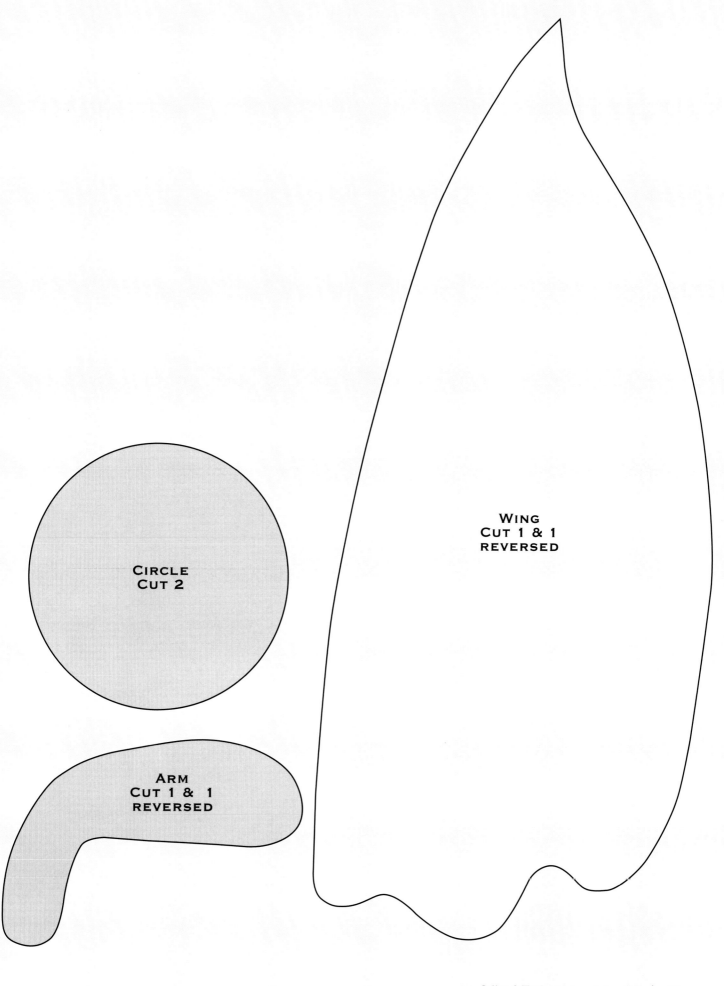

CIRCLE
CUT 2

ARM
CUT 1 & 1
REVERSED

WING
CUT 1 & 1
REVERSED

Saltbox
Size: 24" x 18"

Materials Needed

★ 21 1/2" x 14" soft plaid wool for background

★ 13" x 11" green wool for trees and leaves

★ 12" x 10" red check wool for house

★ Scraps of gold wool for moon, red for tiny hearts and white for 3 stars

★ Scraps black wool for windows, doors and chimney

★ 3" x 24" - 3 colors wool for borders (I used red, navy and black.)

★ Black wool floss

★ Cotton sewing thread to match appliqué pieces

★ 2/3 yard brushed cotton fabric for backing

Sewing Baskets

I have finally figured it out. I buy a new one because I love the design or color or convenience it seems to offer. The last one was a padded basket with lid and sides covered with the black and cream Persian cat fabric. I take a few necessities from the old sewing box and put in the new one, promising myself to keep it neater. The old one, still full of "stuff," is put in a drawer or closet shelf. In approximately a year or so, the new one will be crammed full.

Definition of "stuff" found in old sewing basket

★ Odd safety pins

★ Pencil stubs in a variety of colors and lots of shavings from the pencil sharpener

★ Dirty beeswax, kind of stuck in the corners with pins sticking to it.

★ Fabric ravelings

★ Tangled leftover binding

★ 6 spools colored appliqué thread - tangled together

★ A pair of snippers that will no longer snip at the point

★ 3 sticks chewing gum and some dirty breath mints, one cough drop

★ 2 bandaids

★ 2 small brass screws - where do they belong?

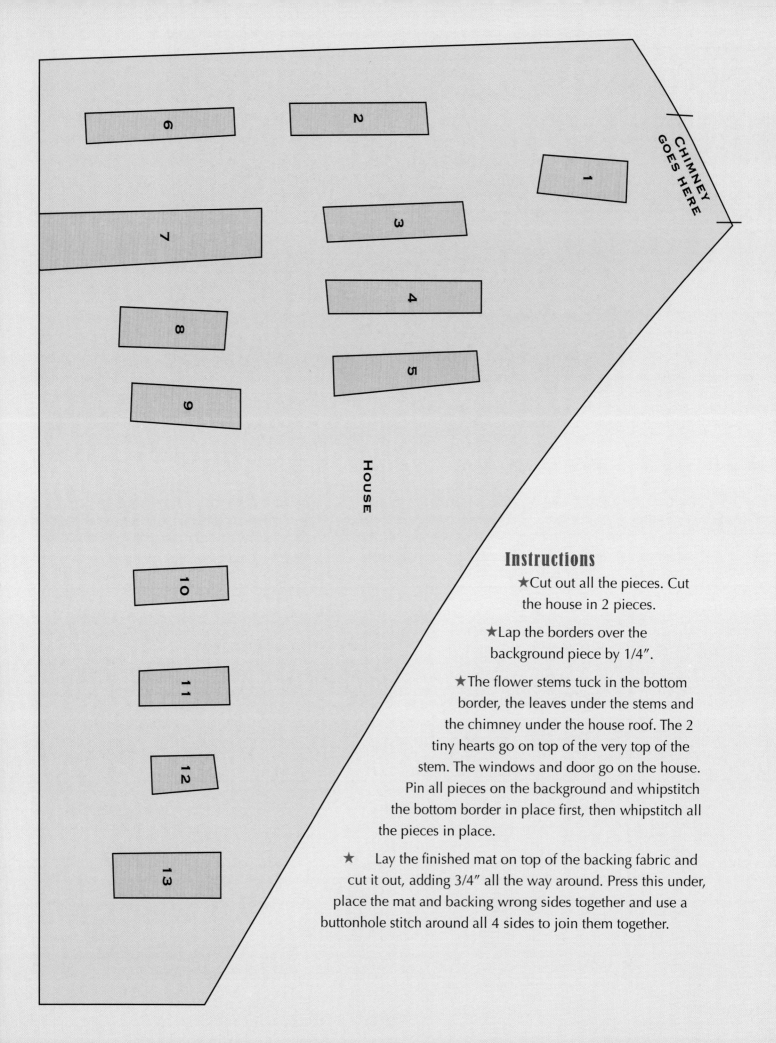

CHIMNEY GOES HERE

6

2

1

7

3

8

4

9

5

HOUSE

10

11

12

13

Instructions

★Cut out all the pieces. Cut the house in 2 pieces.

★Lap the borders over the background piece by 1/4".

★The flower stems tuck in the bottom border, the leaves under the stems and the chimney under the house roof. The 2 tiny hearts go on top of the very top of the stem. The windows and door go on the house. Pin all pieces on the background and whipstitch the bottom border in place first, then whipstitch all the pieces in place.

★ Lay the finished mat on top of the backing fabric and cut it out, adding 3/4" all the way around. Press this under, place the mat and backing wrong sides together and use a buttonhole stitch around all 4 sides to join them together.

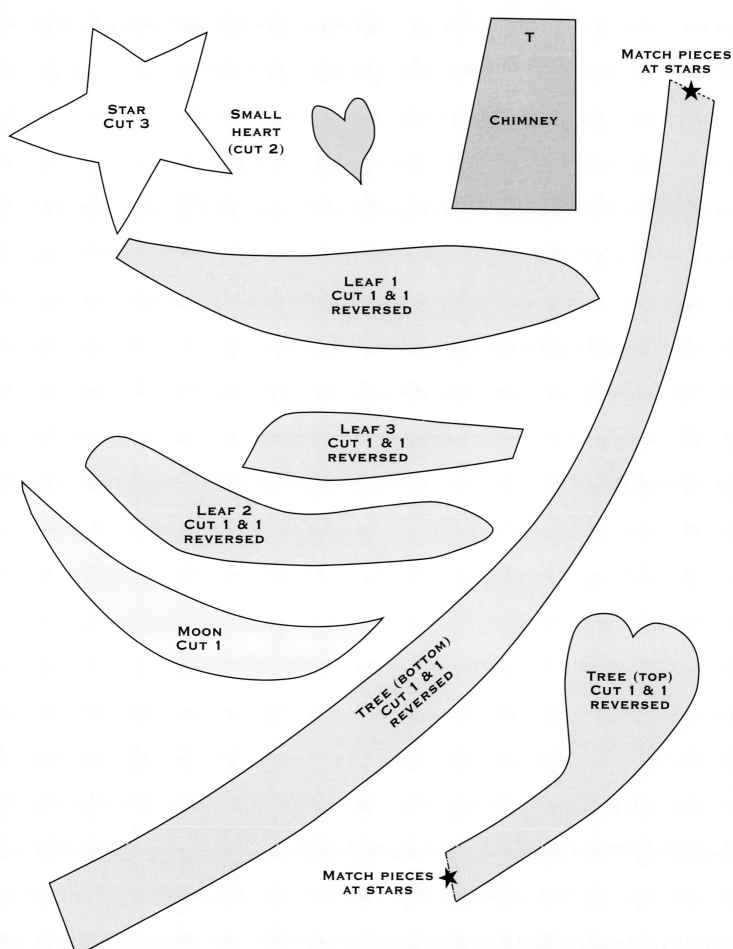

STAR
CUT 3

SMALL
HEART
(CUT 2)

T

CHIMNEY

MATCH PIECES
AT STARS

★

LEAF 1
CUT 1 & 1
REVERSED

LEAF 3
CUT 1 & 1
REVERSED

LEAF 2
CUT 1 & 1
REVERSED

MOON
CUT 1

TREE (BOTTOM)
CUT 1 & 1
REVERSED

TREE (TOP)
CUT 1 & 1
REVERSED

MATCH PIECES
AT STARS

★

Star Pillows
Size: cream colored pillow is 17 1/2" square, white pillow is 15" square.

Materials Needed

Cream Pillow

- ★ Pillow form 17 1/2" x 17 1/2" or cotton or polyester stuffing – whichever you prefer
- ★ Fat quarter of white for background
- ★ Fat quarter cream print for border
- ★ Fat quarter brown/cream print for outside border
- ★ 1/2 yard homespun fabric for backing
- ★ 1 cup mother-of-pearl or white buttons
- ★ 2 1/2 yards medium rickrack
- ★ 1/2 yard flannel, fusible or cotton batting for lining

White Pillow

- ★ Pillow form 15" x 15" or cotton or polyester stuffing – whichever you prefer
- ★ 1/2 yard white fabric for background and backing
- ★ Fat quarter off-white for border
- ★ 1/2 cup mother-of-pearl or white buttons (all sizes up to 1")
- ★ 1 1/2 yards baby size rickrack – cream color or tan
- ★ 1/2 yard flannel, fusible or cotton batting for lining

Character

As the years pass, we grow into our character. I have always said wrinkles and laugh lines add character to our face. When we are young, our faces are a blank map.

When I was shopping at a large department store, I looked in a mirror about a football field away and wondered what my grandmother was doing there. I turned to look - it was me. I always loved my grandmother very much and all the wonderful character lines in her face. I treasure mine since I look exactly like her. The only way to avoid wrinkles is to keep your skin "puffed out." This is also called maintaining a healthy weight. You will notice real thin people always look older than their years (and not as happy). I intend to "puff out" my wrinkles.

Instructions

Cream Pillow

★ Cut background 11 1/2″ square.

★ Cut 1 1/2″ strip for first border.

★ Cut 2 3/4″ strip for second border.

★ Sew borders onto background square, press. Add the flannel or fusible batting, cut the same size as the front of the pillow plus the borders. If using flannel, I pin it together before stitching. If using fusible, fuse according to manufacturer's instructions. Just make sure the sticky side faces the front of the pillow, not the iron.

★ Outline the star shape with a water soluble pen and fill in this outline with buttons. Arrange rickrack around the star 1/2″ away and on the background beside the first border. I stitch the rickrack in place by hand just because I like to do it and I like the way it lies flat. See diagram.

RICKRACK DIAGRAM

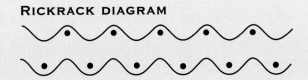

White Pillow

★ Cut background 11 1/2″ square.

★ Cut border strip 2 3/4″, stitch onto all sides and press. Add the flannel or fusible batting, cut the same size as the front of the pillow plus the borders. If using flannel, I pin it together before stitching. If using fusible, fuse according to manufacturer's instructions. Just make sure the sticky side faces the front of the pillow, not the iron.

★ Draw the star with a water soluble pen. Fill in star shape with buttons, then sew the baby rickrack around the background beside the border seam.

Finishing

★ You can either cut backing the same size as the front or you can make an overlap backing with 2 pieces of fabric. Sew around all edges, leaving a 6″ opening, turn and stuff. Either make a separate case for the batting or use a pillow form.

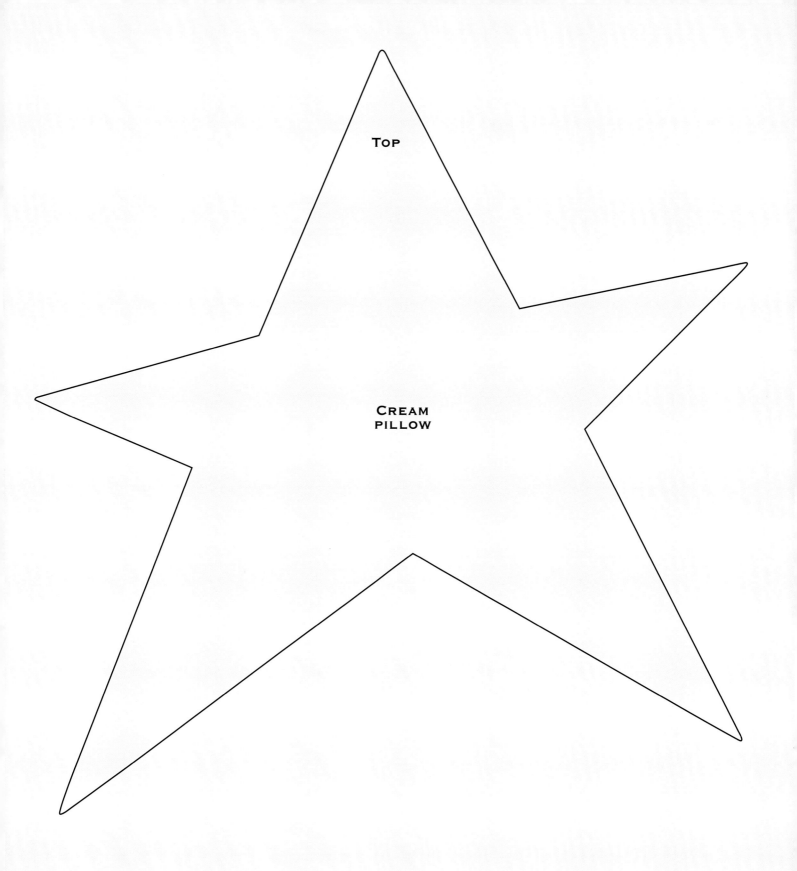

TOP

CREAM
PILLOW

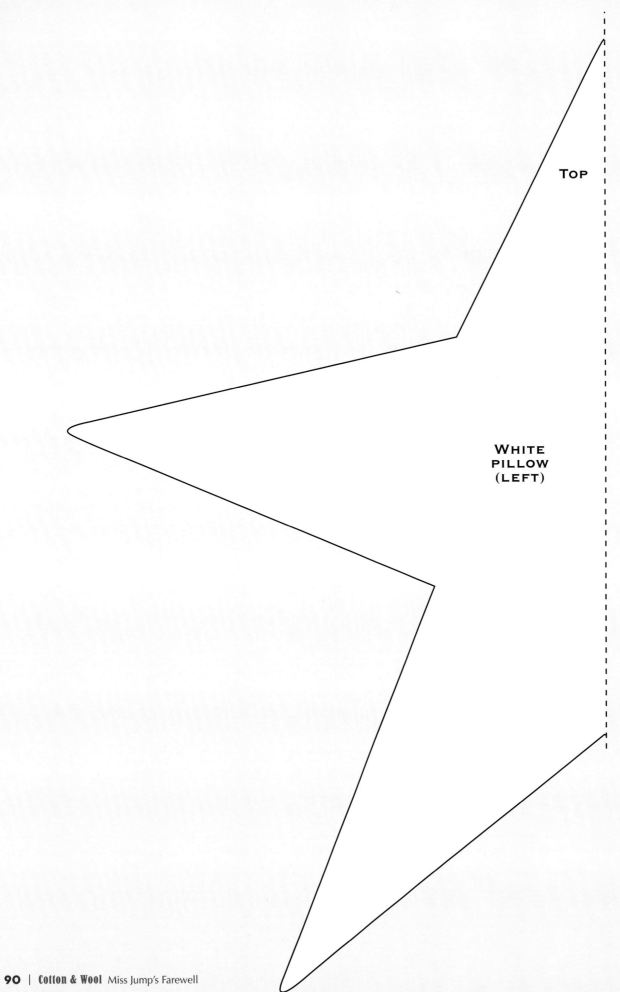

Top

White
pillow
(left)

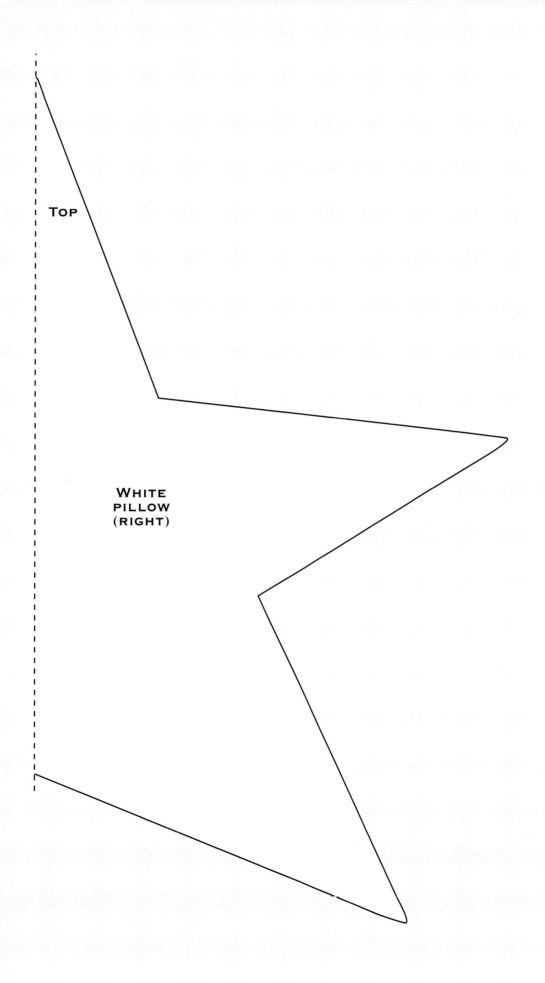

TOP

WHITE
PILLOW
(RIGHT)

American Beauty Hooked Rug
Size: 20" x 45 1/2"

Trees in my Life

The first poem that ever impressed me and I memorized started "I think that I shall never see a poem lovely as a tree." When we bought our home, we had two horrible elms in front. The first priority was to replace them. So, smart us. We chose pin oaks - sturdy, don't break in the wind. Negative side - don't lose all their leaves until spring, have acorns. I like to go barefoot, but you never can under those trees. One year the acorns were so profuse we had to use shovels to get them up.

I have always wanted a bald cypress. They are gorgeous and the leaves are very fine and feathery. Hence, no raking. I finally got a beautiful 7' one. We went to build a screened-in porch and small deck and had to move the tree four feet out. After another year went by, we knew this also was the wrong place. By this time, the tree is 10' tall. We had it moved to the other side of the yard. All was fine.

Then it lost all its leaves in July instead of October. We watched it carefully and then I snapped a branch and knew it was dead. That was ok. I cut off each branch, leaving 12" - 16" and decorated almost every branch with different bird houses, using very small ones at the top. It was great. Guess what? The next spring 11 branches sent out 6 tiny new branches. That was its last gasp. It looks wonderful as a birdhouse tree, although I have not seen a bird use one of the houses yet

Materials Needed

★ 3/4 yard monks cloth with serged edges

★ Wool - 7 backgrounds, gray to yellowish, 1/2 yard each. One background needs to be darker than the rest to contrast with the bowl

★ Black for border 25″ x 25″

★ Yellow plaid for bowl 20″ x 20″

★ Slightly grey for stripe and outline on bowl

★ 4 or 5 reds 15″ x 15″

★ 4 or 5 greens 15″ x 15″

★ 4 yards black rug tape

★ Black wool yarn, 2 or 3 ply (to attach rug tape to rug and protect the edges from wear)

★ Tapestry needle

Instructions

★ Cut all wool strips 3/8″ wide, using an 8.5 blade.

★ You can use freezer paper to cut out the patterns and press them onto the monks cloth. Draw around the shape with a Sharpie fine point permanent marker.

★ If you don't have a rug hooking frame, you can use a wooden quilter's hoop.

★ Hooking is the simple technique of taking a strip of wool in your left hand under the frame and using the hook in the right hand to pull up the strip and make a loop. The height of the loop should be the width of the wool strip. Strive to make the loops consistent and do not pack the stitches too light. This is just like hand quilting for the first time. It feels very awkward and impossible to do. But it gets easier and then it gets fun and sometimes even relaxing. When you have finished the hooking process, trim the monk's cloth to 1 1/2″ from the hooking. Whip on the rug tape, using an overcast stitch very close together so no white monk's cloth shows.

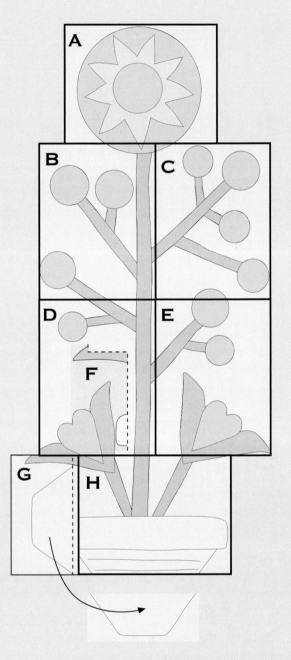

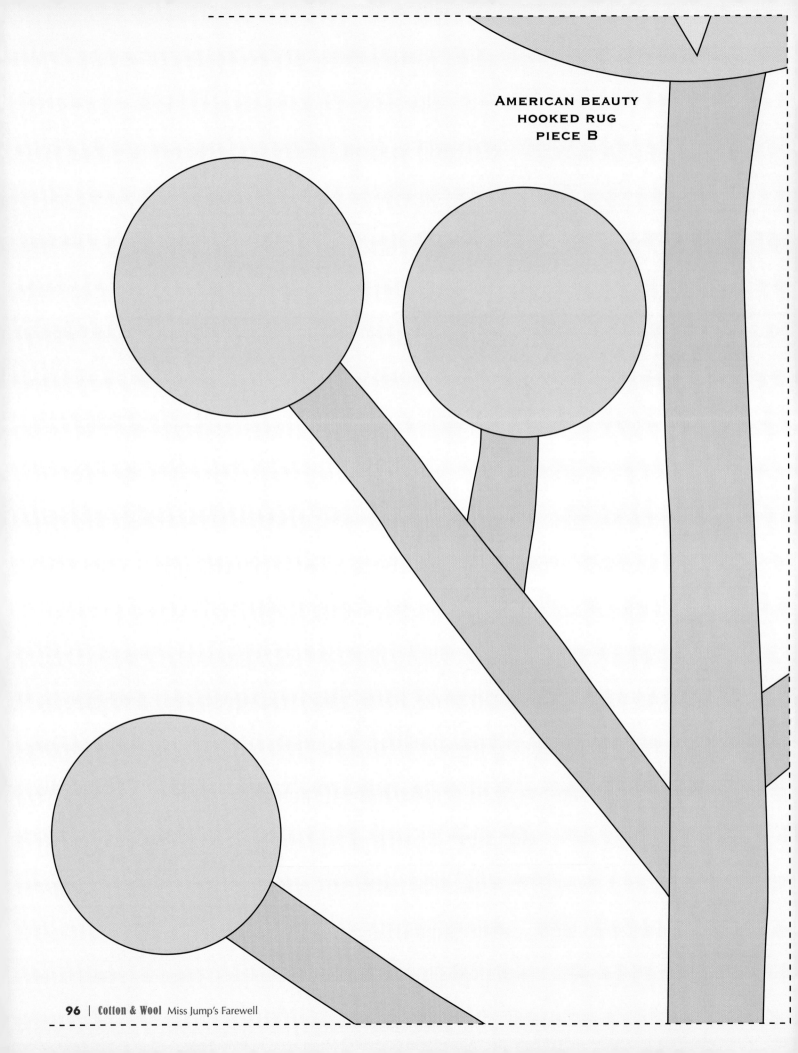

AMERICAN BEAUTY
HOOKED RUG
PIECE B

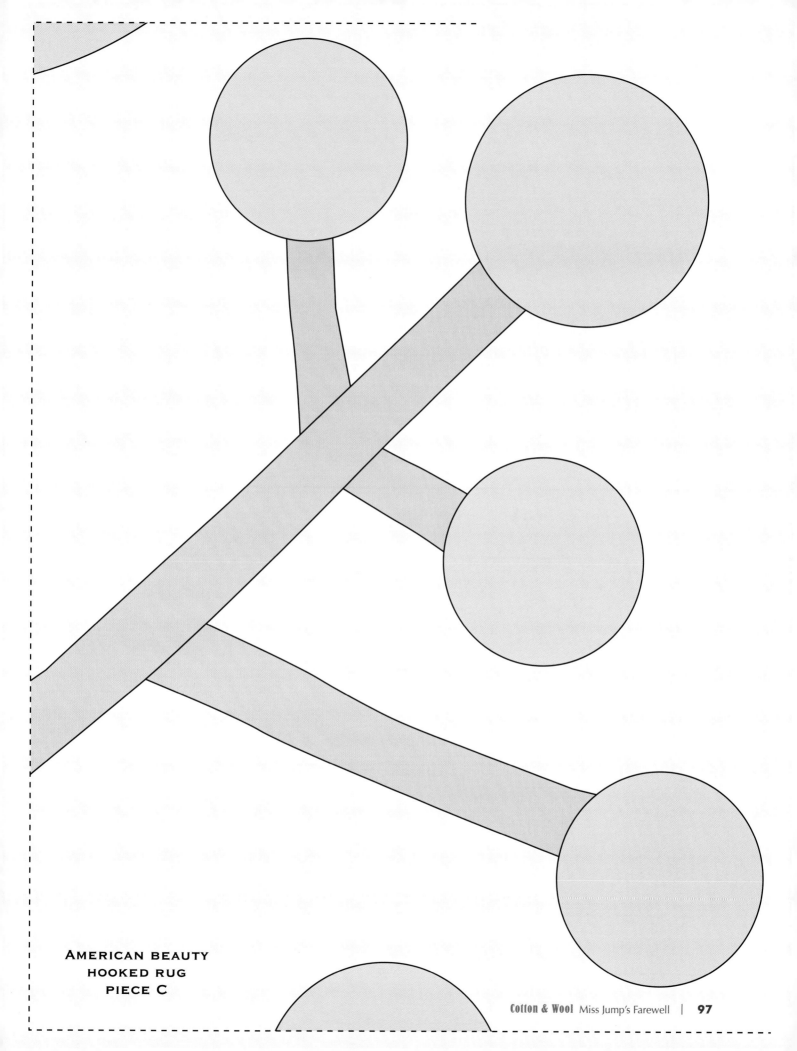

AMERICAN BEAUTY
HOOKED RUG
PIECE C

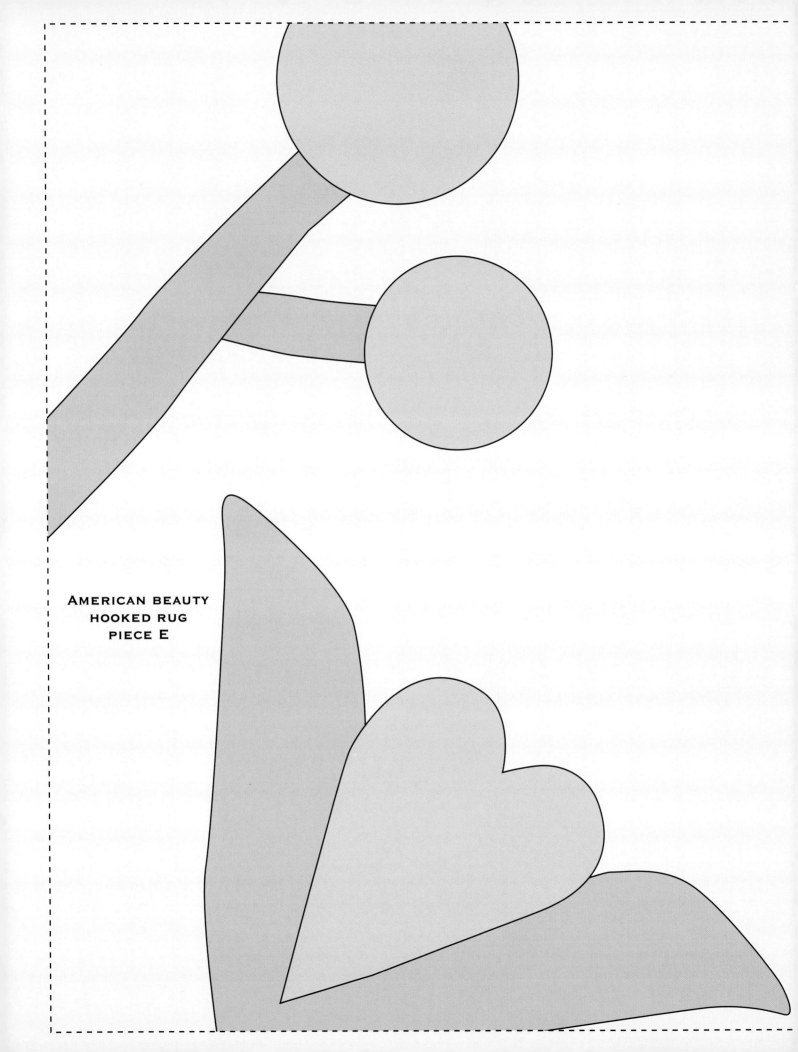

AMERICAN BEAUTY
HOOKED RUG
PIECE E

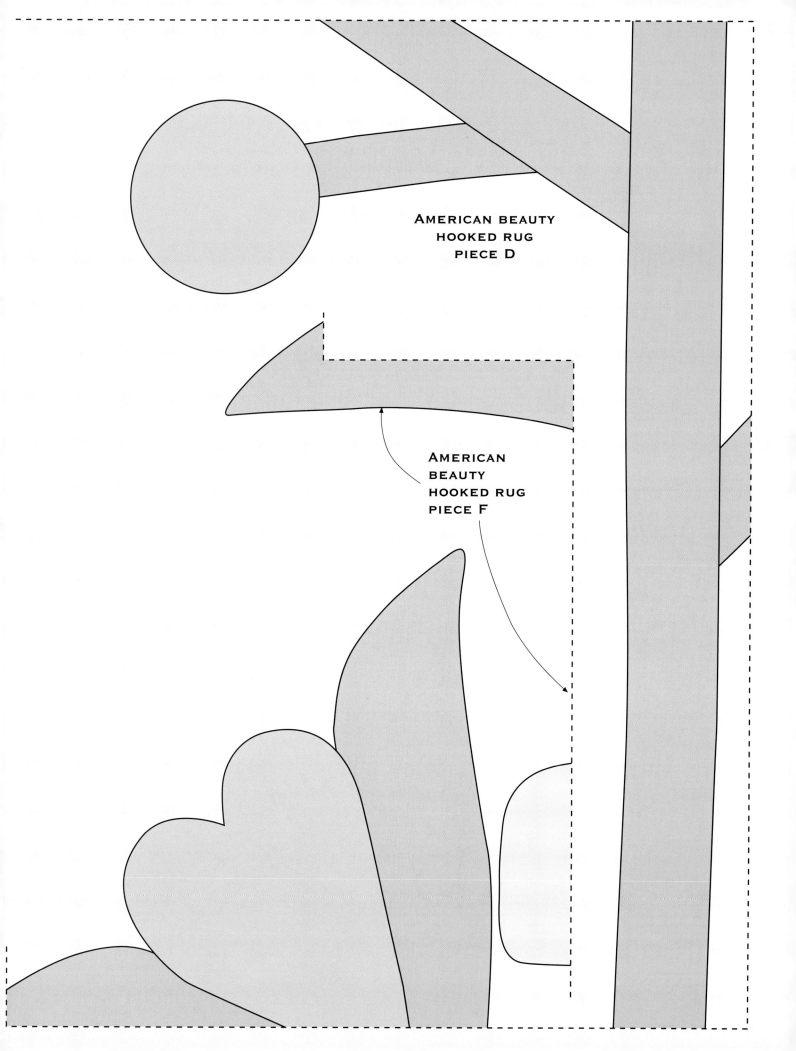

AMERICAN BEAUTY
HOOKED RUG
PIECE D

AMERICAN
BEAUTY
HOOKED RUG
PIECE F

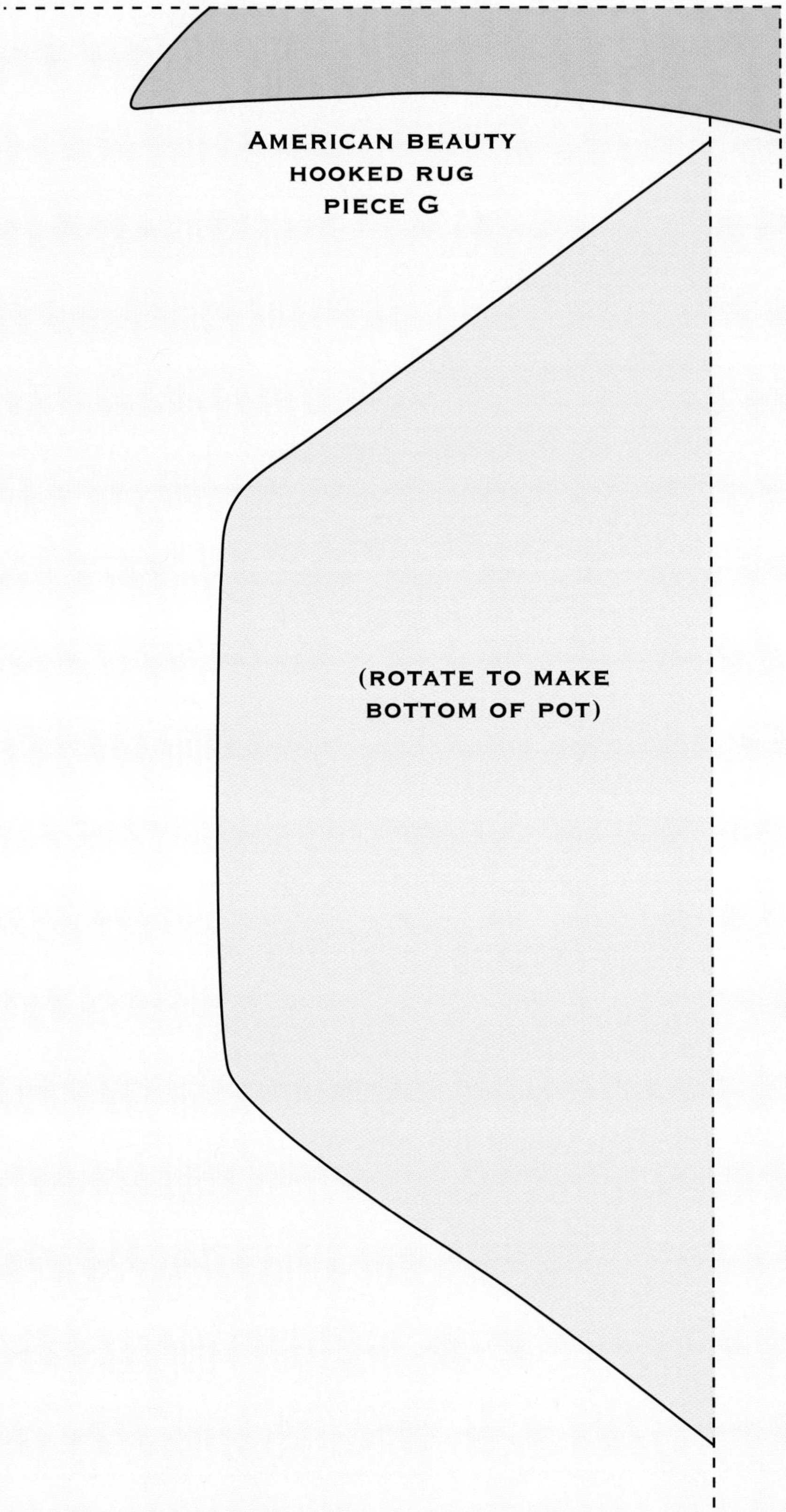

**AMERICAN BEAUTY
HOOKED RUG
PIECE G**

**(ROTATE TO MAKE
BOTTOM OF POT)**

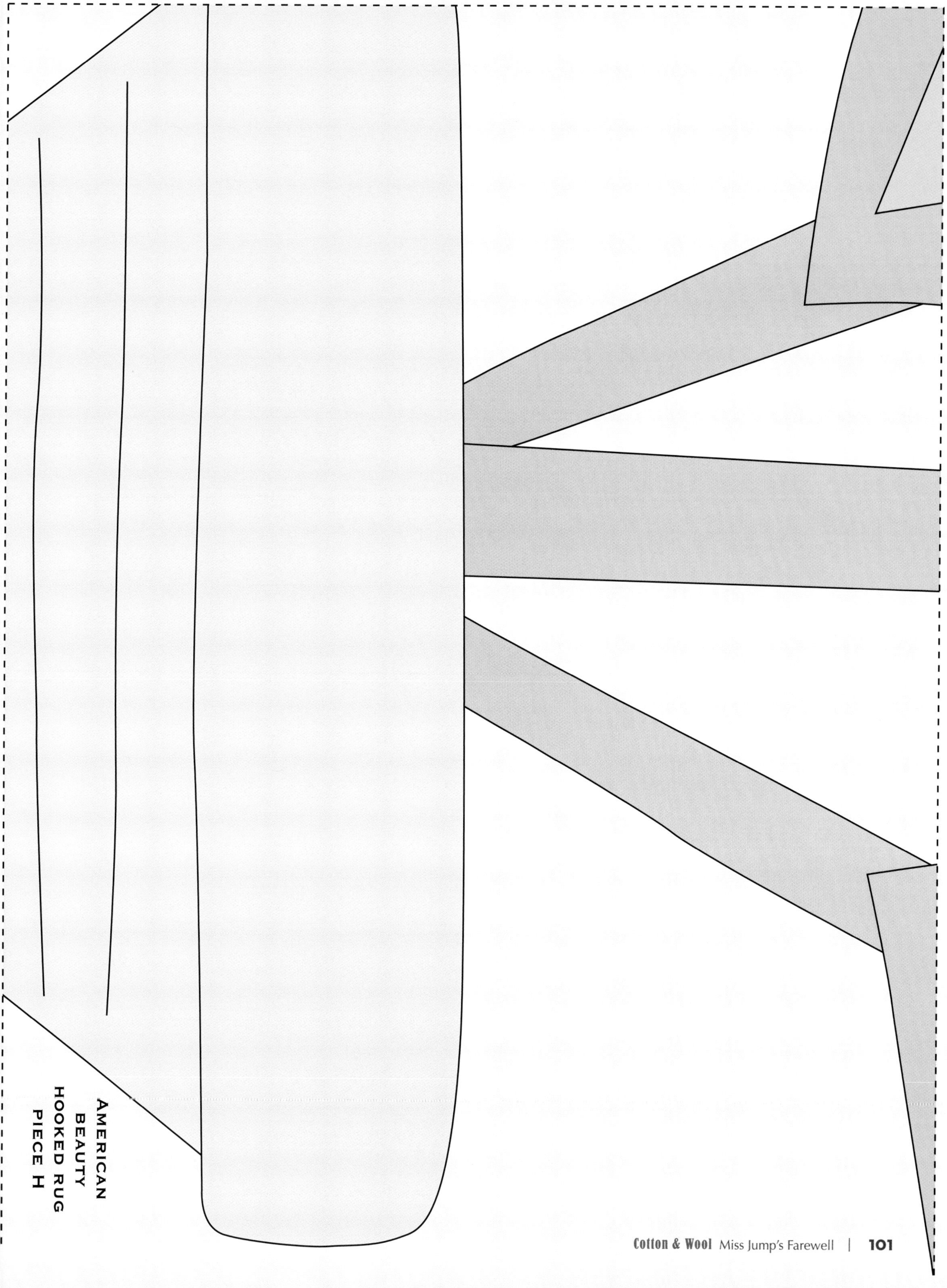

American Beauty Hooked Rug Piece H

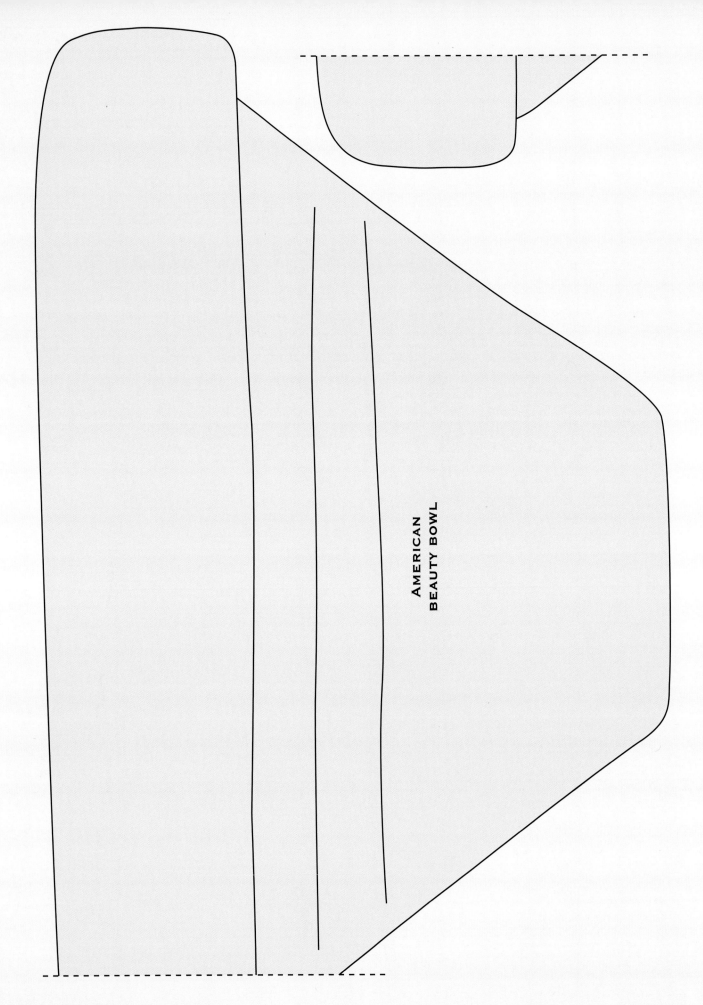

AMERICAN
BEAUTY BOWL

Other Star Books

One Piece at a Time by Kansas City Star Books – 1999

More Kansas City Star Quilts by Kansas City Star Books – 2000

*Outside the Box: Hexagon Patterns from The Kansas City Sta*r by Edie McGinnis – 2001

Prairie Flower: A Year on the Plains by Barbara Brackman – 2001

The Sister Blocks by Edie McGinnis – 2001

Kansas City Quilt Makers by Doug Worgul – 2001

O' Glory: Americana Quilts Blocks from The Kansas City Star by Edie McGinnis – 2001

Hearts & Flowers: Hand Applique from Start to Finish by Kathy Delaney – 2002

Roads & Curves Ahead by Edie McGinnis – 2002

Celebration of American Life: Applique Patterns Honoring a Nation and Its People by Barb Adams and Alma Allen – 2002

Women of Grace & Charm: A Quilting Tribute to the Women Who Served in World War II by Barb Adams and Alma Allen – 2003

A Heartland Album: More Techniques in Hand Applique by Kathy Delaney – 2003

Quilting a Poem: Designs Inspired by America's Poets by Frances Kite and Debra Rowden – 2003

Carolyn's Paper Pieced Garden: Patterns for Miniature and Full-Sized Quilts by Carolyn Cullinan McCormick – 2003

Friendships in Bloom: Round Robin Quilts by Marjorie Nelson and Rebecca Nelson-Zerfas – 2003

Baskets of Treasures: Designs Inspired by Life Along the River by Edie McGinnis – 2003

Heart & Home: Unique American Women and the Houses that Inspire by Kathy Schmitz – 2003

Women of Design: Quilts in the Newspaper by Barbara Brackman – 2004

The Basics: An Easy Guide to Beginning Quiltmaking by Kathy Delaney – 2004

Four Block Quilts: Echoes of History, Pieced Boldly & Appliqued Freely by Terry Clothier Thompson – 2004

No Boundaries: Bringing Your Fabric Over the Edge by Edie McGinnis – 2004

Horn of Plenty for a New Century by Kathy Delaney – 2004

Quilting the Garden by Barb Adams and Alma Allen – 2004

Stars All Around Us: Quilts and Projects Inspired by a Beloved Symbol by Cherie Ralston – 2005

Quilters' Stories: Collecting History in the Heart of America by Debra Rowden – 2005

Libertyville: Where Liberty Dwells, There is My Country by Terry Clothier Thompson – 2005

Sparkling Jewels, Pearls of Wisdom by Edie McGinnis – 2005

Grapefruit Juice & Sugar by Jenifer Dick – 2005

Home Sweet Home by Barb Adams and Alma Allen – 2005

Patterns of History: The Challenge Winners by Kathy Delaney – 2005

My Quilt Stories by Debra Rowden – 2005

Quilts in Red and Green and the Women Who Made Them by Nancy Hornback and Terry Clothier Thompson – 2006

Hard Times, Splendid Quilts: A 1930s Celebration, Paper Piecing from The Kansas City Star by Carolyn Cullinan McCormick – 2006

Art Nouveau Quilts for the 21st Century by Bea Oglesby – 2006

Designer Quilts: Great Projects from Moda's Best Fabric Artists – 2006

Birds of a Feather by Barb Adams and Alma Allen – 2006

Feedsacks! Beautiful Quilts from Humble Beginnings by Edie McGinnis – 2006

Kansas Spirit: Historical Quilt Blocks and the Saga of the Sunflower State by Jeanne Poore – 2006

Bold Improvisation: Searching for African American Quilts – The Heffley Collection by Scott Heffley – 2007

The Soulful Art of African American Quilts: Nineteen Bold, Improvisational Projects by Sonie Ruffin – 2007

Alphabet Quilts: Letters for All Ages by Bea Oglesby –2007

*Beyond the Basics: A Potpourri of Quiltmaking Technique*s by Kathy Delaney – Fall – 2007

Golden's Journal: 20 Sampler Blocks Honoring Prairie Farm Life by Christina DeArmond, Eula Lang and Kaye Spitzli – Fall – 2007

Borderland in Butternut and Blue: A Sampler Quilt to Recall the Civil War Along the Kansas/Missouri Border by Barbara Brackman – Fall – 2007

Come to the Fair: Quilts that Celebrate State Fair Traditions by Edie McGinnis – Fall – 2007

You're Invited! Quilts and Homes to Inspire by Barb Adams and Alma Allen, Blackbird Designs – Fall – 2007

Queen Bees Mysteries:

Murders on Elderberry Road by Sally Goldenbaum – 2003

A Murder of Taste by Sally Goldenbaum – 2004

Murder on a Starry Night by Sally Goldenbaum – 2005

Project Books:

Fan Quilt Memories by Jeanne Poore – 2000

Santa's Parade of Nursery Rhymes by Jeanne Poore – 2001

As the Crow Flies by Edie McGinnis – 2007

Sweet Inspirations by Pam Manning – 2007

Quilts Through the Camera's Eye by Terry Clothier Thompson – Fall – 2007

Resources

Quilter's Station
806 SW Blue Pkwy
Lees Summit, MO 64063
(816) 525-8955
www.quiltersstation.com

Janice Johnson
Wooly Woolens
Blue Springs, MO
(816) 229-2189
http://www.libertyquiltshop.com/wooly%20woolens.htm
jjohnson64057@yahoo.com

Moda Fabrics
www.unitednotions.com

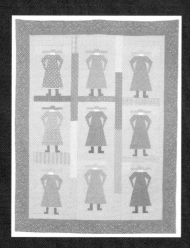